The Curtain Up Players

present

The Handy Book of Unscripted Plays

The Handy Book of Unscripted Plays

Presented by

The Curtain Up Players

(as of March 2017)

Alec Clark
Peter Gray
Joan Gough
Jan Ingham
Linda Jones
Dorothy Leech
Beryl Lockwood
Mike McCormack
Kath Ogden
Christina Wyatt

Editors:
Ron Wiener, Artistic Director
Diane Adderley

No copyright required – please use this material freely to develop spontaneity and creativity in your groups.

ISBN: 978-0-244-35064-2

First Printing: 2017

Published by Diane Adderley, diadderley@gmail.com

Orders:

UK and international orders available from: www.lulu.com

UK orders are also available from Ron Wiener at ron@ronwiener.co.uk

Contents

Acknowledgements

I would firstly like to profusely thank Diane Adderley for putting the book together, for her continual support and professional expertise. I would also like to acknowledge all my psycho- and socio-dramatist colleagues and friends, here and abroad, who have helped me in my development as a sociodramatist.

I want to recognise the immense fun and creativity that I have had with all the actors in The Curtain Up Players over the last eight years of our turbulent existence. I also need to thank those who have helped us on our way such as The Proper Job Theatre Company, Kirklees Council, the Drama and Human Health Science Departments at Huddersfield University, the local branch of Age UK, Kirklees Dementia Action Alliance and the staff at the Brian Jackson Centre.

Ron Wiener
Artistic Director of The Curtain Up Players
Editor

Contact details for The Curtain Up Players

For further information, performances and bookings, see our Facebook page, Curtain Up Players at:

https://www.facebook.com/CurtainUpPlayerstheatre/

or contact us at:

Ron Wiener, Artistic Director at ron@ronwiener.co.uk

Linda Jones, Secretary at wibseyjones@btinternet.com

New members are always welcome.

Foreword

My first encounter with The Curtain Up Players was at an improvised performance demonstration they gave at the University of Huddersfield, as part of an Applied Theatre option on the BA (Hons.) Drama degree, organised by my colleague Dave Calvert. I was impressed by the fluidity, playfulness, and precision of their work. They came across as a warm-hearted and generous ensemble who made the difficult task of improvisation seem easy.

It was my good fortune to be able to join The CUPs a year or so later and improvise in rehearsal and performance with them for several months in the autumn/winter of 2015-16. All the warmth, generosity, and spontaneity I had sensed at the University was present in abundance at each rehearsal and performance and these qualities helped build strong connections with audiences whether the piece being performed was simply a lunchtime entertainment or was exploring difficult relationship issues or illness.

The qualities of the ensemble mean that they are able to adjust to a variety of circumstances and shows can be adjusted at the very last minute when a performer is unable to be involved for whatever reason. Perhaps roles will be switched or the character normally played by the absent actor represented in the third person.

This book offers some of the scenarios and scripts created by The Curtain Up Players: use them as starting points to explore what you want to explore in your own circumstances. They will be useful as starting points for amateur theatre groups as well as school, college and university sessions and group workers of many persuasions.

Franc Chamberlain
Professor of Drama, Theatre, and Performance
University of Huddersfield

July 2017

Introduction

This book contains plays where the scenes are plotted out but characters are free to improvise dialogue. This enables the plays to be used as warm-ups, as a way of stimulating creativity and spontaneity and as a bonus for older actors, where learning lines becomes a problem.

Each section consists of a number of unscripted plays. Each play has a list of characters, together with the scenes, themes that can be explored and aspects of staging. Groups are left free to follow the outlined script or to change any aspect that they wish: characters, scenes or dialogue. Equally, they can change the time frame or the political context.

In the cast lists of some plays, characters have not been given names, simply roles. Those actually on stage are delineated with a capital letter e.g.in *Families*, we have Husband, Wife, Father, Daughter, etc. while those mentioned, but not appearing, do not have capital letters e.g. Daughter's husband is not seen on stage, but is discussed in Scene 5, in the cafe with her Mother-in-Law. In the cast lists of other plays, characters have been given actual names as, in that context, it is an easier way of defining relationships e.g. in *Dinner Party*, it is clearer to say 'Barb and Thomas – Katie's parents', rather than 'Older Husband and Wife – parents of Wife in Host Couple'!

These scripts have a number of advantages over more traditional ones:

- They free theatre groups from having to, yet again, search through the library for plays that have been performed countless times already;
- There is no need to get permission to use the play or to change any aspect of it – in fact, change is encouraged;
- The book will appeal particularly to older people both because there is no need to learn lines and because the process necessitates the ability to improvise creatively and thus to slow the ageing process.

The book is aimed at: amateur theatre groups; school and college drama classes; trainers who need ideas for group warm-ups; and groups for senior citizens who want to retain their spontaneity and creativity.

History

The Curtain Up Players, an amateur theatre group for the over-50s, started off in 2008 as a drama group, the Sunshine Players, based at the Lawrence Batley Theatre, Huddersfield. However, in 2013, we came to a parting of the ways over the direction the group should take and the theatre decided to 'pause' us. Fortunately, we were rescued, in the short term, by the Proper Job Theatre Company, who offered us their rehearsal rooms for a peppercorn rent. We then applied successfully for funds from different Kirklees funding bodies and changed our name to The Curtain Up Players. We moved to a new rehearsal space at the Brian Jackson Centre by the railway station. We now pay a subsidised room rent in return for three performances a year for their luncheon club.

Present situation

The group meets weekly to rehearse on Thursday mornings throughout the year except for breaks at Easter, Summer and Christmas. In 2016, we created eight new plays that we performed in seventeen different locations, including luncheon clubs, care homes, churches and Huddersfield University.

We have worked closely with Kirklees Council, Kirklees Dementia Action Alliance and the School of Human and Health Sciences at Huddersfield University. The last two commissioned a very successful play about dementia and the Herbert Protocol called *Seeking Joan*. We have also performed for local Rotary and Age UK.

For the last two years, we have been funded by Kirklees Council Community Partnerships. However, owing to Government cuts, we have been told that there is no more money for community groups such as ours, so we are now (December 2016) busily seeking funds from a variety of grant-giving bodies. We cover most of our expenses (travel, administration, insurance etc.) from what we charge for our performances. We are short of about £700 a year to cover our rehearsal room rent. There is a limit to what we can charge, as this would mean that we couldn't work with many of the groups who support older people, who also have limited funds.

Environment

We live in a time where older people are living longer but not necessarily in conditions conducive to a good quality of life. There is austerity and cuts to many benefits, though older people, in terms of pensions, have perhaps done well, in comparison to younger people. However, this doesn't take into account cutbacks on local government adult social care services, such as home helps and other community support bodies: for example, the closure of local libraries. Care homes are under financial pressures and many offer poor quality of care with little for residents to do.

The Curtain Up Players' Social Capital

Over our eight years of existence, we have built up considerable social capital: friendship bonds, which help combat isolation, have helped people through the death of partners and parents and in their role as carers. Some people stay for lunch after session, phone each other up in between sessions and meet for lunch. We are aware that this can make it difficult for newcomers to join and we try to set up a buddy system wherever possible.

What worked against this was that, with an older cast, there were rarely any rehearsals where all were present. People were either sick, caring for relatives, waiting in for workmen or on holiday during school term-time, when fares were cheaper.

When developing a play, we would start with an exchange of ideas, which would then develop into a series of short trial scenes, until we arrived at something we all felt we could work with. Once we had agreed on the characters and who might play them, we would usually do some 'hot seating' (the actor playing the role answers questions from the rest of the cast about their life while staying in role) to develop back-stories.

We would end up with a series of scenes within which actors were free to extemporise. We needed to be clear how a scene would end in order to cue exits and entrances.

In between performances, we would develop the spontaneity of group members (the ability to go 'yes and...'), often by starting a story in between two members and then involving other members, who had to build on the scene that was developing.

Staging

The plays had to be capable of performance with minimum sets, as we frequently found ourselves in settings without a stage or, if there was one, there would be no backstage area or just one set of stairs or a possible exit room being used as a store cupboard. Also, we had little money for props or set designs. This was intentional: we wanted to keep our cost base as low as possible so that we could continue to function even if grant funding disappeared.

Audiences

Our audiences have ranged in number from a dozen up to 200. In care homes, the struggle was sometimes to keep people awake and engaged. When performing to professional audiences, it was to entertain and inform, as it was for luncheon clubs and other semi-public shows.

On all occasions, we would try to involve the audience wherever possible. In care homes, we would use songs and bring along props that people might remember from their younger days. On other occasions, we would have actors in the audience who could interact with them (see *Seeking Joan*, for example).

Allied Groups

We are closely linked with a group in Leeds, which I also direct, called Don't Act Your Age, based at '7', a community arts centre. This group is also for the over-50's but is a social improvisation group rather than a performing group.

We also have a sister group in Warwick, New York State whose director, Linda Richmond, is establishing a further group in Atlanta.

Postscript – September 2017

We have just learnt that we have new funding for the next twelve months to work with the local Asian community to translate some of our dementia plays into Urdu and Punjabi and find a group of actors to deliver them in local settings to raise awareness of dementia in the Asian community.

We have also been approached by Kirklees visually impaired groups to produce a play that will highlight, to the wider population, issues faced by members of the group.

So, as we go to press, we are moving into another development phase. We hope that this will also lead to us being able to recruit more new members to the group.

You can find out what happened next by following us on Facebook where there are also videos of some of our performances.

Enjoy.

Ron Wiener
Artistic Director

SECTION 1: Family Relationships

1. Modern Dating

2. Families

3. The Quiz Show Audition

4. The Dinner Party

5. Marriage Lines

6. The Spare Room

1. Modern Dating

The idea for this play came from the T.V. programme 'First Dates'. It was first performed at the Huddersfield Central Library for one of their regular coffee mornings.

Cast

Man

Woman

Man's Wife

Man's Mate

Man's Mum

Woman's Friend

Woman's Daughter

Woman's Mother

Scenes

The play is a series of scenes with two characters on stage at any one time, who are then replaced by two more characters.

1. Man and Woman meet face to face in a café after hooking up on the internet. They have an introductory chat then leave.

2. Going back in time, Woman is talking to her Friend about her fears and hopes of going on the date.

3. Man talking to his Wife, from whom he is separated, about how both are dealing with their separation and what the boundaries are.

4. Woman talking to her Mother about how she and her father met, exploring dating habits in previous generations.

5. Man talking with his Mate about going on this date – male banter.

6. Woman talks to her Daughter, who tells her mum about the dangers of internet dating, with implicit young person's disgust that their parent might be sexually active.

7. Man talks to his Mum. Mum expresses her disappointment with her son, who is not sticking by his marriage vows.

8. Man and Woman have more of a chat getting to know each other. Man goes to the toilet.

9. Woman speaks to her Friend on the phone (actors sit back to back) about how the date is going. Man comes back. Woman says it is her turn now to go to the toilet.

10. Man speaks on the phone to his Mate. Woman comes back. Mate leaves.

11. Man and Woman finish. (It was left up to the two actors each time to decide whether their relationship was going to continue or not.)

Possible themes to explore

- Dating across generations
- Male v female hopes and experiences of dating
- Difficulty of dating as one grows older
- Risk of STDs and how to talk about contraception

Staging

Props – all that was needed were two chairs.

Man and Woman had a lot of freedom as to how they would play their characters and what their back-stories were.

2. Families

This play was commissioned by the Packhorse Gallery in Huddersfield for Mental Health week. The play explores some of the stresses in families that can lead to problems such as depression.

Cast

Husband

His Wife

Her Father

Their Daughter

G.P. (female)

Husband's Boss

Daughter's Mother-in-Law

Manager of the Care Home

Neighbour

Alternative therapist

Scenes

Scene 1: Husband and Wife's home

On stage: Husband, Wife and her Father, who has come to live with them after his wife's death. Their Daughter has also returned home, having separated from her husband. She is not on stage at the beginning.

Father spends most of this scene dozing. Husband and Wife argue over living arrangements, to include:

- Husband is not sleeping or eating well because of the number of people in the house;

- Wife's sleep is disturbed because she can't move into the spare bedroom if her Husband is fidgety in the night;
- Husband wants to know how long Father will be staying.

Daughter enters at this stage and wants to know if she is going to be thrown out too, arguing that it's not her fault that her relationship has broken down. Her father reassures her that she can stay as long as she needs to. Reassured, she goes off to have a shower.

Father wakes up, wanting to know what the fuss is about. He is also reassured – told it is nearly time for dinner. He goes off to lay the table.

Wife persuades Husband to see his G.P. for something to help him sleep. They leave to go to the kitchen.

Scene 2: Doctor's surgery

On stage: Husband, Wife and G.P.

Wife is talkative about the home situation; Husband is more guarded.

G.P. probes to find out what the problem is.

Husband asks Wife to leave; she does so, reluctantly.

Husband tells G.P. about a possible erectile dysfunction problem.

G.P. prescribes a short dose of sleeping pills. She also suggests counselling, but says there is a long wait for an appointment.

Husband leaves.

G.P. stays for a moment typing up her notes before she also leaves.

Scene 3: Husband's workplace

On stage: Husband and his Boss

The Boss is unsympathetic. Husband's work is slipping and if he doesn't pull himself together sharpish he will be made redundant.

Scene 4: Back at home

On stage: Husband, Wife, Daughter and Father

Daughter asks about the visit to the doctors.

Wife emphasizes the importance of Husband keeping his job to get him out of the house and for their finances.

Issue of whether Daughter should get back with her husband.

Husband and Daughter fall out.

Daughter says she is going to meet her Mother-in-Law.

Husband goes upstairs for a lie down.

Wife and Daughter exit to the kitchen, off stage, for a cuppa.

Scene 5: In a café

On stage: Daughter and her Mother-in-Law

Daughter tells Mother-in-Law about her issues in living with her husband.

Mother-in-Law says her son gave her everything.

Daughter says she might have had a lot of material things but her life was empty and boring. Her husband was always out with his mates playing sport. She has been to her G.P. and is on anti-depressants.

Scene 6: Back at home

Husband has asked the Manager of a nearby care home, to call in.

Husband wants to know the feasibility of Father going into the care home.

Care Home Manager extols the virtues of her care home.

Interrupted by Wife coming in with her Father. She is furious with Husband for doing this behind her back. While they are arguing, the Care Home Manager slips out.

Daughter comes in and wants to know what is happening.

Husband is harassed and looks like he might be losing it.

Scene 7: At home

On stage: Wife and her Neighbour

Neighbour is being helpful about Wife's worries about Husband, but she says all the wrong things about mental health. Neighbour is into meditation and mentions that there is an Alternative Therapist at the local community centre.

As she is leaving she mentions that she has seen Husband having a piss in his back garden.

Neighbour leaves. Wife picks up a paper but moves around anxiously.

Husband enters. Wife starts getting at him, telling him that she knows he has lost his job and has been pretending to go to work. Husband is angry, saying he told her not to phone him at work. She mentions the pissing incident: he says what do you expect with so many people taking so much time to use one bathroom. Husband is distraught: Wife persuades him to go and see the Alternative Therapist.

They go and get a cuppa.

Scene 8: In the Therapist's room

On stage: Husband and the Alternative Therapist

Alternative Therapist overplays the role but includes some good sense.

Tries meditation on doubting Husband, who tries unsuccessfully to sneak out.

Leaves with a classical tape.

Scene 9: Back at home

On stage: Husband, Wife and Daughter

Father has moved into the care home – Husband visits regularly.

Husband is feeling better.

Daughter is beginning to lose it – she is developing a drink problem. She leaves to have a bath.

Wife and Husband reminisce about the good old days and end up planning a weekend away.

They leave to find brochures.

Possible themes to explore

- Family dynamics under stress
- Mental health system under pressure
- Attitudes towards mental health
- Role of alcohol
- Prevalence of anti-depressants
- Loneliness in older people
- Critique of materialism
- Difficulty men have in 'fessing up to life-changing events

Staging

We only used four chairs and a table, changing the position of the furniture for different scenes, and used a different tablecloth for different locations.

G.P brought a laptop with her. Alternative Therapist had some scarves and music.

3. The Quiz Show Audition

Cast

Family One: The Ramsdens

    Betty, Mrs Ramsden

    Florence – Betty's mother

    Arthur, Mr Ramsden – Betty's husband

    Janice – Florence's sister

Family dynamics – Florence and Janice are sisters who don't get on. Betty, Florence's daughter, is married to Arthur, who doesn't get on with Florence, his mother-in-law. Janice has a soft spot for Arthur, which fuels her strife with Florence.

Family Two: The Postlethwaites

    Paul – Simon and Roger's father

    Roger – married to Veronica

    Simon – married to Carol.

Family dynamics – Simon is henpecked by Carol but supportive of her in public. Roger is Simon's bossy older brother. Roger is critical of his wife Veronica's relationship with his father Paul. Veronica criticises Roger for not spending enough time with his dad. Veronica and Simon get on OK. Veronica doesn't rate Carol's intelligence – only knows price of everything in the supermarket. Carol was the family member who suggested they should enter the competition.

Toby Lerone, the Quiz Show Host,

Scenes

Scene 1

Toby comes on stage chatting to the audience explaining that they are the audience at a quiz show audition. There will be two families and their task will be to decide which one will go through to appear in the actual programme. They need to decide which family is the most telegenic, not necessarily the one who answers the questions best. Toby then leaves to bring in Family One.

Scene 2

Toby comes back in with The Ramsdens, who squabble over seating arrangements. He gets Janice to introduce the family members to the audience. Family members say a little about themselves which produces some surprises for other people in the family. There is family discord. Toby leaves to sort out refreshments. More family discord. Toby comes back on and leads the family offstage to get the refreshments.

Scene 3

Family Two, The Postlethwaites come in from the opposite side of the stage. They say this is where they have been told to wait. They squabble. They acknowledge they are in front of an audience but can't stop arguing among themselves.

Toby comes back on. Apologises for not being there. Gets Roger to introduce the family members. They each say a bit. Roger tries to bribe Toby to include his set of questions. Toby leaves to get Family One, The Ramsdens. More family discord between The Postlethwaites.

Scene 4

Toby returns with The Ramsdens. The Postlethwaites notice the other family have refreshments which they themselves haven't been offered. They protest about this.

Then it's quiz time. Each family is given a question in turn and there is internal discord as to who has the right answer. Toby asks easy questions to The Ramsdens and more difficult ones to The Postlethwaites, which fuels inter-family arguments. Conflict ensues within families, between families and with Toby. If no team gets the right answer, Toby has the option of involving the audience.

Scene 5

Toby, at the end, turns to the audience and gets their vote. He can, of course, disregard the popular vote and nominate whichever family he wants to win, giving the possibility of more discord in between and within families, both when the result is announced and with Toby himself and, finally perhaps, between Toby and the audience. Eventually the families leave, Toby thanks the audience and also leaves the stage.

Possible themes to explore

- Various aspects of family life
- How quiz/TV shows are geared towards entertainment – aspects of the post-truth society.

Staging

Obviously, the basic structure is simply to allow the arguments within and between the two families. Therefore, groups are free to create their own families.

Props – again very simple: 10 chairs plus some refreshments for Family One, The Ramsdens.

4. The Dinner Party

Cast

Andrew and Katie – host couple

Liz – single person invited by her friend Katie

Barb and Thomas – Katie's parents. Thomas is hard of hearing, mishears words

Malcolm – old friend of Andrew's, who has been invited as a dinner companion for Liz. Works in menswear, lives with Derek

Scenes

1. Andrew and Katie on stage as a couple about to welcome their guests. Some bickering, Andrew is sent off to change.

2. Liz arrives – has a conversation with Katie which establishes their relationship.

3. Barb and Thomas arrive. Katie and Barb go offstage to the kitchen; Liz and Thomas talk.

4. Andrew, Katie and Barb all reappear and Malcolm arrives.

5. Andrew accompanies Thomas to the toilet, Barb and Katie go back to the kitchen. Malcolm moves and sits next to Liz.

6. Noises offstage as Andrew asks Thomas if he is OK on the toilet.

7. Malcolm and Liz talk. Malcolm gives an impression that he might be gay, at least this is Liz' assumption.

8. Liz goes to join the women in the kitchen.

9. Andrew comes back in and talks to Malcolm. They then go offstage to get drinks for everyone.

10. Liz, Katie and Barb come back in. Barb continues off-stage to see where Thomas is.

11. Barb and Thomas come back in.

12. Katie runs to the kitchen because there is a smell of burning cabbage.

13. Andrew and Malcolm come back in. Andrew goes to the kitchen to see what is happening. Malcolm tries again with Liz.

14. Andrew comes back in, says dinner is ruined and he is going for a takeaway. Katie is in the kitchen clearing up the ruined dinner.

15. Liz and Malcolm talk more. Despite first impressions, Liz realises Malcolm is straight – they decide not to wait for the takeaway and they sneak out.

16. Thomas is feeling woozy – Barb takes him off stage for a lie down.

17. Andrew and Katie burst into an empty room with the takeaway.

18. Barb re-enters – explains what is happening with Thomas and leaves to continue to look after him.

19. Andrew and Katie argue. Andrew leaves for the pub.

20. Katie sits and eats a poppadum on her own. She is then silently joined in turn by Barb, then Thomas, then Andrew and then Malcolm and Liz, who are holding hands. They all pick up a poppadum as they enter.

Possible themes to explore

- Andrew and Katie's rocky relationship, one aspect of which is her cooking.
- Comic possibilities:
  - Thomas being hard of hearing
  - Thomas on the toilet
  - Malcolm giving Liz cause to assume he is gay
- Malcolm and Liz and the problems of middle-age dating
- Difficulties of being a carer – Barb and Thomas' relationship
- Maintaining dignity in public in old age – Thomas / Andrew
- The importance of women's friendship – Katie / Liz

Staging

Very simple set – one table, six chairs

5. Marriage Lines

Commissioned in 2017 by the Elderberry Group

Cast

Julie and Alistair – long-married couple

Kylie and Cath – their daughters

Malcolm – Cath's husband

Paul – Malcolm's friend

Scenes

Scene 1

Julie and Alistair on stage discussing:

A marriage that has drifted – somewhat friends, no longer lovers;

How they met 50 years ago

They leave.

Scene 2

Cath and Malcolm are sitting on a train discussing their approaching visit to Cath's parents. He is not keen on his in-laws. Cath wants to know why he has been having so many late nights. Malcolm, who is a director of a double-glazing company, says they are just business calls. Malcolm says that when they get to the station he is going to visit an old friend first and will join Cath later.

They leave.

Scene 3

Kylie and Cath – Julie and Alistair's daughters are sitting in the car outside their parents' house. Kylie, who has never married and lives in the same town as her parents, has picked up Cath from the station. They discuss:

Cath's worries that husband Malcolm is having an affair – suspicious briefs, perfume etc. – also includes a discussion about thongs;

Cath asks Kylie not to tell their parents.

They leave.

Scene 4

Malcolm meets Paul in a pub. Malcolm talks about his marriage to Cath and temptations that come his way to be unfaithful. Is ribbed by Paul.

They leave.

Scene 5

Julie and Alistair on stage discussing the impending visit.

Kylie and Cath appear – greetings – then Kylie blurts out that Cath has something to tell you. Cath angry with Kylie – just jealous because she has a husband – parents embarrassed but eager to know more.

Cath says Malcolm is also here and will drop in.

Malcom appears – tense atmosphere – women go off to have tea in the kitchen.

Scene 6

In the kitchen daughters are supportive of Mum having some time for herself – they suggest going on a holiday to Spain.

They leave.

Scene 7

Alistair and Malcolm have a man-to-man chat – women reappear – Cath accuses Malcolm – he says he is blameless but has had enough of always being in the wrong – Malcolm storms off. Kylie and Cath leave to go to a travel agent to see about the holiday.

Scene 8

Malcolm reappears in the pub complaining to Paul about what has happened. He phones Cath to say he is going to stay at Paul's house tonight. Cath *(on side of stage)* says that in that case he needn't bother coming back to their house in Grantham. Malcolm complains to Paul that he is now homeless. They leave.

Scene 9

Julie and Alistair compare their marriage to single daughter Kylie's life and to Malcolm & Cath's. Decide their marriage could do with spicing up – off to buy new underwear.

They leave.

Possible issues to be explored

- Sibling rivalry
- Sex and old age
- Adultery
- Male bonding
- Men's emotional communication inadequacies
- Marriage and changing expectations over time

Staging

Straight forward – five chairs that can be rearranged from Alistair and Julie's living room to the different scenes – the train, the car where Kylie and Cath are sitting and the pub scene.

In the pub scene, we used two beer glasses as a visual prompt.

6. The Spare Room

This is an updated version of the first play ever performed by the company at the Lawrence Batley Theatre on the 11th December 2007.

Cast

Mary and Fred – an old married couple

Louise - their 24-year old married daughter

Adam - Louise's husband

Brenda – Mary and Fred's estranged daughter

Florence – Mary's mother

Scenes

Mary and Fred's house. Mary and Fred are discussing what to do with their spare room. Mary wants a sewing room, has never had a room all to herself. Fred saying you've had the whole house while I was working. Fred, now he has retired, wants the room for his hobby, model trains. Raises the whole issue of retiring man getting on wife's nerves by being around all day and not having anything constructive to do that compensates for what they got from work.

Mary leaves to visit her mother, Florence, who lives alone and whom she is worried about – is getting very forgetful etc.

Fred goes to have another look at the spare room.

Scene 2

Florence sitting alone in her house, knitting, under dressed – Mary enters – greets her – is alarmed at how cold her mother is – puts a cardigan on her mother – asks her why she hasn't switched her fire on – Florence is in a bit of a daze – I'll do it now – nearly trips as she gets out of her chair – Mary rushes to help her – notices a half-eaten sandwich – asks if that is all Florence has had to eat – Florence says she wasn't hungry – Mary says come with me and takes her off stage to the kitchen

Scene 3

Adam and Louse's house. Early evening. Louise is marking some papers, listening to the radio. Adam comes in and switches the radio off. Louise reacts angrily. Adam says he has had a bad day at work and can't tolerate any noise, just wants peace and quiet. Louise – what about what I want or need. It's always you, you – obviously an ongoing argument that just continues to escalate that finishes with Adam storming off to the pub and Louise saying don't expect me to be here when you get back.

Scene 4

Back in Mary and Fred's house – Fred sitting there alone, reading the paper – Mary comes in and says we need to do something about my mother:

Mary:	She can't live on her own anymore – she'll have to move in here, into the spare room.
Fred:	*(protesting)* It can't be that bad, what about you going and visiting her more
Mary:	It's two bus rides away
Fred:	What about home helps?
Mary:	The council don't provide them anymore unless you're really desperate.
Fred:	I've set my heart on having that room – you're always telling me to do something to get out from under your feet.
Mary:	It doesn't have to be in the house – go and play bowls or something.

The phone rings – Mary answers (Louise appears at the side of the stage) – a short discussion in which Louise says she and Adam have had a major argument and can she come and stay for a few days

Mary: Yes, not sure, I'll have to ask your father – hang on for a moment.

Fred: Who's that?

Mary: It's Louise – she and Adam have had another argument. She wants to come and stay with us for a bit.

Fred: You know my view – once you've made your bed you need to stay lying in it.

Fred likes Adam and argues that Louise should stay with him, as he and Mary did through their ups and downs.

Mary: I'm not always sure that's for the best – anyway divorce was frowned on in our days – lots of people have second or third marriages these days.

Fred: Well she's not coming here tonight and that's final.

Mary: You tell her then – I'm going to get a cuppa. *(exits)*

Fred: *(picks up phone and walks off stage)* Hullo love, terribly sorry but your mum's not well – let's leave it for tonight – and we'll talk about it in the morning.

Scene 5

Brenda sitting at home doing her nails – knock at the door and Louise enters:

Brenda: What are you doing here? You never visit?

Louise talks about her relationship with Adam – how self-centered he is and how she needs to get away – wanted to go to mum and

dads for a few days to use the spare room but dad put her off –
never expected that.

Brenda: You never come and suddenly you expect me to be
               all open arms and meet your needs.

Louise: Well you have a spare room.

Brenda: Shows how little you know – I've sub-let that for the
               last three months – anyway our parents aren't the
               sweet little couple they pretend to be with you – one
               day I'll tell you the story of why we don't get on any
               more and then you'll see them in a new light.

Louise: Can't I at least have the sofa for tonight?

Brenda: Just for tonight. Come on, I'll get you some
               bedding.

They leave.

Scene 6

Next morning. Fred and Mary are sitting at home, drinking a cup of
tea, continuing the argument about who should have the spare room
– Mary says perhaps Louise should have it to make up for the past
– just for a few days – Fred against it.

The phone goes – Fred answers – yes … no … not since last night
… will do.

He hangs up.

Mary: Who was that?

Fred: It was Adam wanting us to tell Louise that it's over
               as far as he is concerned. Appears Louise won't
               speak to him to-day.

Mary: Where was Louise last night then?

Fred: According to Adam, she stayed at Brenda's.

Mary:	That won't do – she'll just get bad advice there – she'll have to come and stay here.
Fred:	What about your mum?
Mary:	It will only be for a few days.
Fred:	Not if Adam meant what he said, anyway I don't want either of them here – Louise is old enough to stand on her own feet.

Mary interjects talking about the housing situation and how lots of people in their twenties are now living with their parents.

Fred:	Not like that in my day – and I couldn't stand your mother here day after day wittering on.
Mary:	Well I can't cope with you blathering on all day.
Fred:	Well I'll go to the shop then and get the paper.
Mary:	You do that.

He leaves – Mary picks up the cups and leaves the other way.

Scene 7

Florence is sitting at home – knitting – still under-dressed – Louise enters.

Louise:	Hi Gran
Florence:	How nice of you to call – it seems a long time since you were last here.
Louise:	Gran, I have a favour to ask you – can I sleep in your spare room for a few days.
Florence:	Yes, but – it's full of all my possessions.
Louise:	It would only be for a few days – I could help you move them.

Florence:	No dear, I know where everything is – I wouldn't want anything touched – I have everything just as I need it.
Louise:	But Gran …
Florence:	No dear – it just wouldn't do but stay and have a chat – I do get lonely when no one calls.
Louise:	I'd love to but I have so much to do.

Louise leaves.

Florence sits dejected then leaves, trailing her knitting behind her.

Scene 8

Fred and Mary are sitting – Fred reading his paper – Mary a magazine. There's a knock on the door and Brenda appears – Fred and Mary both startled.

Fred:	We didn't expect to see you
Mary:	Come in.
Brenda:	I'm going to Australia in a few weeks to travel around for a year.
Mary:	But that's so far away.
Brenda:	What difference will that make to you?
Mary:	Don't be like that.
Brenda:	How do you expect me to be?
Fred:	What do you want?
Brenda:	I just thought there might be a final chance to make some peace before I went but not if you speak like that.
Fred:	Your poor mother worries about you all the time – she's always thinking about you.

Brenda:	A pity then she wasn't like that years ago when I needed her – It wasn't my fault that I got pregnant and then you wouldn't let me keep her – I just wanted you to help look after her but no, you made me have her adopted – I've been looking for her for years but there's no trace and you expect me to be grateful – fat chance
Mary:	But they were hard times and you were still at school and your dad …
Fred:	Don't blame me – you didn't want to look after her either.
Brenda:	No wonder I never come round – look can't you at least let me leave some of my stuff in your spare room while I've gone. I've left the flat to my tenant and she has a friend moving in while I'm away.
Fred:	We'll think about it.
Brenda:	That's what I thought would happen – I haven't asked you for anything for years and you can't even do this for me.

Turns and leaves

| Mary: | *(to Fred)* What have we done? |

They leave.

Scene 9

Adam at home – pacing around – Louise enters.

Adam:	You're back?
Louise:	Just to pack.
Adam:	Don't be hasty – I'll try to change, do better.
Louise:	Too late.
Adam:	Where will you go?

| Louise: | Alice at work has a spare room, she said I could stay with her for a while – she would be glad of the company and someone to help pay the rent – you know what it's like these days – I'll just go and pick up a few things – I'll be back in a few days to gather the rest of my things – then you'll have a spare room. |

Louise leaves. Adam picks up his phone, dials a number.

Adam *(leaving the stage as he talks):* Mike, Adam here – how do you advertise a room on AirBnB?

Possible themes to explore

- Loneliness of old people
- Changing attitudes to pregnancy
- Problems of young people being unable to afford to buy houses
- Marital disharmony
- Need financially for both people in a relationship to work while the woman is still expected to do the majority of the housework.

Staging

We used different throws to indicate different settings.

Props: radio, newspaper, knitting, a magazine

SECTION 2: Christmas Shows

1. Two Linked Plays:

    i. The Choir

    ii. The Choir's Xmas Panto

2. Santa's Factory

3. What If Pantomime

4. Finding Cinderella

5. The Women's Institute Pantomime

1. Two Linked Plays

i. The Choir

The Choir was first created for a performance in November 2016 for the Meltham Friend to Friend luncheon club. We then needed to create a play for the Brian Jackson Centre luncheon club in December that had a Christmas theme, so we adapted the play into *The Choir's Duet Contest*, which gave us the opportunity to include a lot of Xmas carols that the audience could join in with. We were then invited to do a pantomime for the Kirklees Older Person's Network, so *The Choir* got adapted again and became *The Choir's Xmas Panto*. In keeping with our normal style none of the showings slavishly followed the text as written.

The aim in including *The Choir's Xmas Panto* here is to show how any of the plays can easily be adapted, depending on the needs of the performance.

Cast

Husband and Wife

Divorcée

Spinster

Old Bachelor and his next door Neighbour

Choirmaster

Newcomer to village who wants to audition

Scenes

For clarity, as characters enter the stage, they are represented in capitals.

Scene 1

CHOIRMASTER on stage, setting out the scene for the choir's third meeting – he is a bit of a bumbler who is fairly new in the village. He goes out to the kitchen to check on the boiler.

HUSBAND and WIFE come on – arguing about Xmas arrangements and also Husband wants Wife to audition for the choir (she hasn't been before). Their arguing touches on past issues in their relationship. It's important to the Husband to make things right with his Wife – he sees her doing well in the choir as something that will achieve this.

CHOIRMASTER comes back in. Husband introduces Wife. Choirmaster says there is a problem with the boiler – Husband and Wife go with him to look at it.

DIVORCÉE and SPINSTER come in talking (setting the scene for their relationship). Divorcée is touchy, twice married, sexually adventurous; Spinster is uptight, sexually naïve, doesn't like being touched – Divorcée wants to help Spinster with her coat but she refuses.

BACHELOR and his NEIGHBOUR come in, making their relationship clear. Bachelor needs help but still wants his independence while Neighbour wants to help. Her possible motives are money and companionship.

CHOIRMASTER, HUSBAND and WIFE reappear – Wife gets introduced.

Moves immediately into Scene 2.

Scene 2

Choirmaster attempts to take charge – discussion about what songs to sing. NEWCOMER enters, asks if she can join – discussion and disagreement re whether there needs to be an audition. Some disagreement among choir members but audition takes place. Newcomer does well, Wife doesn't and is upset at being embarrassed in public – Husband suggests 'you can always make the tea' – Wife rounds on him for suggesting that that is all she is good at and storms off. Husband goes after her.

Choirmaster suggests that they all go and have a cup of tea.

They all leave for the kitchen except for Bachelor and Neighbour, who again squabble over their relationship but eventually go off into the kitchen

Moves immediately into Scene 3.

Scene 3

Different combinations of people come onto stage with cups of tea.

DIVORCÉE and SPINSTER have their conversation, highlighting their different attitudes towards life, finishing with who will have Bachelor for Xmas dinner – Divorcée suggests they have a bet as to who can snare Choirmaster. They leave to get another cuppa.

HUSBAND and CHOIRMASTER come on – Husband persuades Choirmaster, for the good of his relationship, to give Wife another chance – suggests she could read a poem instead – Choirmaster agrees. They leave to check the boiler is still working well.

NEIGHBOUR and SPINSTER come on. They have a serious conversation about Xmas loneliness – Spinster leaves to get another cuppa. BACHELOR wanders back on.

Neighbour and Bachelor reach some sort of compromise.

CHOIRMASTER and NEWCOMER have a conversation which suggests that they might become a couple – DIVORCÉE and

SPINSTER come onto stage at the side or back and realise that their cause is lost – Choirmaster and Newcomer leave to round up the others – Divorcée and Spinster find a way of visiting each other over Xmas.

Others join them on stage.

Moves immediately onto Scene 4.

Scene 4

Choirmaster calls everyone to order – explains about Wife – gets her to say her poem – then says choir needs to practice a couple of songs *(*we used *Oh Come All Ye Faithful* and *Rudolph the Red-nose Reindeer).*

Choir sings one song through first, then Choirmaster invites audience to join in as they sing it through again.

Possible themes to explore

- Loneliness
- The difficulty men can have in expressing their emotional needs.
- The pressures of Xmas on family relationships.
- Different values in relation to 'having fun'.

Staging

We had the pairs come on stage for their first entrance through the audience speaking about their relationships.

Simple set: seven chairs.

ii. The Choir's Xmas Panto

This is a continuation of the play *The Choir*. The choir is rehearsing again after Christmas.

The indented sections in italics in the text indicate how the play was adapted after the first performance ready for the next performance.

Cast

Choirmaster

Newcomer

Husband

Wife

Divorcée

Spinster

Bachelor

Neighbour

Scenes

Scene 1

Need to make relationship between Newcomer and Choirmaster more central in the play

CHOIRMASTER and NEWCOMER come on stage reminiscing about their time together over Xmas

Need to expand this a bit e.g
Newcomer: When you came for Christmas, I never thought it could come to this – but you

*turned out to be the best Christmas present
ever.*

Choirmaster: The fairy on the tree ...
More like Santa on the rug...
Making sweet music together ...etc.

*Choirmaster hopes they have been discreet, because he is
worried that it will affect things in the choir if everyone
knows about their relationship.*

Newcomer reminds Choirmaster of the song he sang her on New
Year's Eve and gets him to sing it again — he sings 'You are my
Sunshine'

Choirmaster reminds Newcomer that they have been asked by the
village to put on a pantomime. He has contacted everyone over
Xmas to ask them to come up with their ideas for the panto. He
says he wants to put on Snow White and has ideas for the roles
people could play. Newcomer should play Snow White and he will
be Prince Charming. He then suggests that they go and put the
boiler on. They leave singing 'You are my sunshine'.

Scene 2

HUSBAND and WIFE come on stage arguing.

*Need to expand this e.g. how Wife burns his toast – You'll
give me cancer (recent story in the press linking the two)*

*Link to a long-standing argument about not having
children: Wife is sad.*

*Husband: I never wanted anyone but you – I didn't
want to share you*

Husband wants to play Aladdin and thinks Wife could be his lamp.
Wife doesn't want to be in it.

Wife: I'm always rubbing you up the wrong way.

CHOIRMASTER joins them. Husband explains his plan for the panto. Choirmaster says he already has a role for them in Snow White. Husband could be the Wicked Queen.

Husband: I'm not playing a woman. There's nothing female about me.

Wife still doesn't want to be in it.

Choirmaster suggests she could be the mirror.

Wife and Husband think this is a good idea.

Some opportunity to play "He's behind you" as they try out the suggested roles.

Wife: I just have to tell him he's the most important person in the world, so what's new.

Husband is still not happy but is persuaded by Choirmaster to come and have a cuppa. They all leave.

Scene 3

DIVORCÉE and SPINSTER come on, talking about what happened over Xmas.

> *Need to make more of how Spinster was this shy uptight person and how that has changed — perhaps Divorcée saw Spinster having a snog with her brother at the New Year's party and Spinster didn't realise she had been seen. In performance, the two actors improvised that Divorcée's brother was gay and that Spinster hadn't realized.*

They then talk about having agreed to do Cinderella and then the different roles they could take on – Spinster as Cinderella, Divorcée as Fairy Godmother.

CHOIRMASTER comes in: I thought I heard voices. Most of the others are having a cup of tea. I need to tell you about the pantomime.

Spinster and Divorcée: We have to tell you about our ideas first.

They do so.

Choirmaster says no they are doing Snow White and he has cast them as dwarfs. Asks which one would suit them – some disagreement over which dwarf role would suit them

> *Need to expand this*

Opportunity for "Oh no, we're not – Oh yes you are".

Choirmaster: Let's discuss it further over a cup of tea.

They leave.

Scene 4

BACHELOR and NEIGHBOUR come on – talk about Xmas – Bachelor had gone round to Neighbour's for Xmas dinner but then left to go to the Legion. They remain friends, but Bachelor wishes it had gone further.

They talk about panto – he wants to be Captain Hook

Neighbour suggests she could be Tinkerbell, much to Bachelor's amusement, which upsets her. He tries to pick her up which she rejects.

CHOIRMASTER comes back on – they talk about Peter Pan – Choirmaster says no, it's going to be Snow White and he has Bachelor down as a dwarf and Neighbour as a huntsman.

Neighbour objects as she is a vegan – looks to Bachelor to support her. He doesn't. She gets angry with him for being a poor friend and storms off.

Choirmaster is critical of Bachelor but then says we'd better go after her as we need her in the panto.

They leave.

Scene 5

SPINSTER and DIVORCÉE return. They squabble over the Snow White role.

Eventually decide to get Wife, as the mirror, to help them decide. They call for WIFE who enters.

> *As Wife comes in Divorcée is giving Spinster a hug*
> *Wife complains about not getting any hugs etc*
> *Spinster: Even though you are married to (Husband)*
> *Wife just shrugs sadly – i.e. it's Husband's fault she is childless*

They do "Mirror, Mirror on the wall"

Wife hears Spinster ask the question, then replies: Next!

Then Divorcée asks and Wife replies: I'll have to ask my Husband.

They all leave moaning about Choirmaster's decision to put on Snow White and how Newcomer has got the role of Snow White when she has only been in the village for two minutes.

Scene 6

HUSBAND and BACHELOR come back. Husband thinks he should be Prince Charming rather than Choirmaster. Thinks about what can they do about it. Has the idea of going on strike.

Bachelor points out that there is no Prince Charming in Snow White.

Husband: Oh yes there is

Bachelor: Oh no there isn't

Husband: I'm not having any of it.

Bachelor: That's what the story is back stage.

Husband gets angry about this – who said that? – she has no right to talk about my life …

He is cut short by...

SPINSTER and DIVORCÉE return. Husband explains his idea. They agree to support him.

CHOIRMASTER and NEWCOMER come on looking a bit dishevelled, as if they have been having nooky offstage somewhere.

> *2nd performance – they walk on silently together through the audience. Comments from those on stage.*

The group argue that they are going on strike

More "Oh no you're not ..Oh yes we are".

They complain about Newcomer being Snow White. She is caught between her relationship with the Choirmaster and her need to be accepted by the others if she is going to settle in the village.

Newcomer agrees to join the protestors. This leads to an argument between her and Choirmaster.

Issue about past relationships

Newcomer: I bet you've tried it on with other people in the choir.

Divorcée blushes. Newcomer sees this and accuses Choirmaster.

Divorcée: It was only once.

The rest turn on Divorcée except for Husband who tries to make peace. Gets everyone to come together.

Then there is a crash and WIFE enters

Wife: I have broken the mirror.

Neighbour: That's seven years bad luck.

Husband: What have you been saying about our marriage?

Wife: Nothing.

Choirmaster: Well, there's no time left today to work out which panto we're going to do. Let's finish with a couple of songs the audience might know.

Choir sings, encouraging audience to join in, 'You are my Sunshine' and 'Happiness, happiness'

Possible themes to explore

- Family relationships
- Friendships
- Old age dating
- Conflicts in choirs

Staging

Minimal props: the different actors who played the Bachelor, when talking about playing Captain Hook, used the end of a coat hanger and a walking stick for a hook.

2. Santa's Factory

The stage was set up with a series of work tables that the audience were invited to sit at. On the tables are a set of cheap props that can be used to make Christmas toys.

Cast

Father Christmas (referred to as 'FC')

Mrs. Father Christmas (referred to as 'Mrs. FC')

FC's Ex-Wife

Nurse

Worker

Builder

Foreman (female)

'Elf & Safety Inspector (referred to as 'H&S') (female)

Parent

Scenes

1. FC greets the audience as they arrive and sends them to sit at the tables where WORKER and BUILDER are already seated.

2. FC then greets the workers – telling them they are unemployed people sent from job centres in England to help him with the Christmas rush as there are no jobs back home. If they are good workers he might keep one or two on a permanent basis.

    FOREMAN arrives and calls for silence:

    WORKER: Who are you?

FOREMAN: The foreman.

WORKER (aside): Funny looking man.

FOREMAN says they need to be creative and make do with what's on the table e.g. turning toilet rolls into binoculars because FC is also suffering from an economic crisis. Tells them to get on with it and leaves to her office (on separate part of stage).

3. FOREMAN joins FC in his office. Their conversation covers how FC has lost his money in a bad investment (Ponzi scheme / internet scam / banking crisis). Therefore there is no money for new toys. FC says they are behind schedule – FOREMAN must get them working harder.

4. FOREMAN comes back out to tables – tells workers they must work harder. WORKER protests about the working conditions; wants a H&S inspector. FOREMAN leaves.

5. H&S comes on – is horrified – puts on long gloves and removes toilet rolls – WORKER says he has hurt himself – H&S says she will get the nurse. She leaves.

6. NURSE appears – WORKER takes the opportunity to complain about his assessment back in England – says he should have been registered as disabled and not sent to work – NURSE is sympathetic and says she will see what she can do. She leaves.

7. H&S appears in FC's office – she complains about the poor state of the toys. FC says what can he do – he is broke. H&S leaves.

8. Mrs. FC joins FC having walked down through the tables – she is good looking and dressed provocatively. There are wolf whistles (*opportunity for discussion re sexual harassment*). Mrs. FC is uninterested in her husband's financial difficulties – she is only interested in her spending allowance (*possible discussion re celebrity culture and gold-diggers*).

They argue. She leaves angrily when she doesn't get any money.

9. Mrs. FC flops into an empty seat next to the WORKER who asks her what's up. She says she has a fiscal problem with her husband which the WORKER hears as 'physical' and says he can help and starts to offer her inappropriate advice. She gets angry again and storms off.

10. NURSE reappears in the office. FC talks about his 300-year history and how he has had ten wives during this time – none of them have given him the problems the present one has. His new problem that he shares is that he now realizes that he has become scared of chimneys. They discuss ways of dealing with this. FC leaves to take a pill that NURSE suggests might help.

11. BUILDER enters the office – he is overweight and this is creating a problem as he often helps FC by driving the sleigh – they discuss problems of obesity – NURSE gives him some advice – he leaves.

12. H&S enters the office to say she is feeling depressed as she is retiring after Christmas – they have a discussion re retirement, old age etc. They leave to have a cuppa.

13. BUILDER and FC re-enter the office. They talk about how the BUILDER might lose his job unless he loses some weight. Raises issue about redundancy.

14. PARENT appears at the other end of the stage at an imaginary door and rings a bell. FOREMAN enters office and tells FC there is a parent to see him. A bit of physical farce as he has to insert pillows to create his image. FC then becomes 'Jolly Santa' as he hurries down the aisle. PARENT complains to Santa about how she and her son have been treated in a store. FC explains that it is a franchise business and he can't be held responsible for what happens at all the outlets. PARENT, unsatisfied, leaves.

15. In FC's office. Mrs. FC appears and phones Harrods to order a new expensive dress. EX-WIFE appears. Mrs. FC looks guilty. EX-WIFE says not to worry – he's always broke and anyway your time is nearly up – every 30 years he trades us in for a new model. It's the first time Mrs. FC realizes how old Santa is – she is disgusted at having married such an old man – EX-WIFE leaves going down the aisle in between the tables – meets up with FC, who asks her what she thinks of his present wife – EX-WIFE challenges him for his male menopausal behaviour – she continues out off stage. FC, stressed, continues to his office.

16. FC and Mrs. FC have another blow up about money and his age – Mrs. FC leaves threatening to tell the real story about Santa (discussion includes a bit about alternative facts) – she leaves talking into her mobile phone.

17. FOREMAN enters office – FC asks her to get the workers to work harder. FOREMAN leaves – goes to the workers and says they need to produce more – WORKER say no – (possible yes/no pantomime sketch) – WORKER gets the other workers to down tools – FC comes out – FC throws a wobbly – says he will call Christmas off – just a way for everyone to make money except for him – 300 years is quite enough – he tells the workers to go and leaves and sits in his office. Workers amble off stage while FOREMAN comforts FC in his office.

18. Cast come back on and sing a Christmas song.

Possible themes to explore

- The economic crisis that creates the unemployment was what was around at the time of writing. Two years later ,one could include Brexit / immigrants / zero hour contracts / the gig economy etc.
- Similarly, FC's economic crisis as to how he has no money – Brexit / trade barriers / tariffs etc.
- WORKER's possible disability could open up a discussion on how people with disability are treated generally in terms of benefits and particularly in assessments about being fit for work.
- BUILDER's possible redundancy leads to discussions about the decline in trade union power and the difficulty in older people finding work.
- H&S's retirement creates space for all the themes about ageing to be explored.

Staging

The stage setting with audience involvement was only possible because we knew the size of the expected audience. With a slightly bigger cast there would be no need for audience involvement. Alternatively, it could be staged with no workers and the play could be set in the time while the rest of the cast were waiting for them to arrive.

Props: we needed a large number of scrap props – discarded old toys, felt, scissors, bits of lego etc. for the workers to play with.

We had three tables, each with five chairs. The office at one end of the stage simply had one table and two chairs.

3. The 'What If ...' Pantomime

This performance was put on for Age Concern in Huddersfield.

Cast

Dick Whittington (DW)

His Mother

Aladdin

Hansel and Gretel's Witch

Sleeping Beauty

Cinderella

Jack

Ogre

Red Riding Hood (RRH)

Goldilocks

Snow White

Scenes

Scene 1

SLEEPING BEAUTY is asleep on a bench on one side of the stage.

DW and MOTHER appear on the other side. They argue – she thinks he is too immature to go to London – he's just a silly little boy. DW carries some bread and cheese and a spare pair of under-pants in a knotted red handkerchief on the end of a stick which he shows to his mother,

They see SLEEPING BEAUTY – DW wants to wake her up – MOTHER says to let her sleep – their argument wakes her up.

SLEEPING BEAUTY is very angry – it has taken her months to get to sleep and she has to sleep for a hundred years before she is woken by a handsome Prince – they have ruined her chances. DW offers to kiss her to save her going back to sleep – she rejects his offer as he is no handsome Prince – MOTHER angry with DW for offering to kiss SLEEPING BEAUTY.

CINDERELLA appears – she is fleeing London after marrying her Prince. Life was not happy ever after. She is disillusioned with life in the royal household – all the hunting, shooting and dressing up. The press, no privacy, too much ceremony, bitten by corgis and the streets are not paved with gold. CINDERELLA tries to tell SLEEPING BEAUTY that it's therefore pointless trying to get back to sleep to wait for a Prince because all men are useless liars – faint protest from DW.

MOTHER offers to take CINDERELLA and SLEEPING BEAUTY home for a good cup of tea.

Scene 2

DW sits down on the bench to have his bread and cheese before continuing on to London when ALADDIN arrives.

ALADDIN turns out to be a refugee – word play on 'asylum' and 'genie / Jeannie' – he was dropped at a service station where he lost his lamp and got parted from Jeannie – thinks the lamp might have been stolen – how can he survive without them – wants DW to come and help find them.

GOLDILOCKS appears clutching a heavy bag – sits down on the bench – she starts telling the story about the three bears. ALADDIN is worried about bears and thinks he might have seen GOLDILOCKS before somewhere. DW wants to know what's in the bag – GOLDILOCKS is defensive – there is a struggle – bag spills open – out drops some silver and ALADDIN's lamp. GOLDILOCKS confesses she is a sneak thief and has burgled the three bears' cottage. ALADDIN is happy to have his lamp back. ALADDIN and GOLDILOCKS recognize that they are both con people and GOLDILOCKS agrees to be his new genie. They practice on DW who gets fooled. The two leave, laughing.

Scene 3

DW gets ready to start off when JACK appears, running and out of breath. He is a timid mummy's boy, who went up the beanstalk looking for some playmates but slipped and fell when he heard an OGRE calling 'fee-fi-fo-fum' – he looked up to see the OGRE climbing down the beanstalk and he has been running from him ever since. Sound of 'fee-fi-fo-fum' coming closer – audience "He's behind you" – JACK runs off – OGRE appears and DW stops him, asking why he is chasing JACK – OGRE says he is lonely and wanted JACK as a friend – leaves chasing after JACK. DW picks up his swag and disappears off stage. JACK reappears, exhausted, and sinks to the ground – OGRE comes back on stage – JACK – please don't hurt me – OGRE says he just wants a friend – they talk, then leave stage hand in hand.

Scene 4

RRH appears – sits down – WITCH comes on stage – RRH tells her story about fleeing from the wolf while on her way to take food to granny – she is tired of being a young carer, life should offer more. WITCH is sympathetic – says she is looking for Hansel and Gretel – her dear children who have got lost – she asks if RRH would help her look for them (all the time sliding down the bench to be closer to RRH) – says if we can find them then we can all have a meal together (RRH moves down the bench away from the WITCH). DW appears – RRH takes opportunity to flee.

DW becomes therapist to the WITCH: Why don't you lie down on the bench and tell me what's troubling you – WITCH talks about escaping from the oven – looking for Hansel and Gretel – is she bad or is she bound by her genes to act this way – there is a family history of eating children – nature v nurture – DW believes she can change – oh yes she can / oh no she can't – she goes off looking for Hansel and Gretel – unresolved whether she is going to say sorry or eat them.

Scene 5

SNOW WHITE appears, on her way to start a new life – has had enough of serving seven small men – plays on their different attributes with strong sexual innuendos. She chats up DW – invites him to go with her to a small flat she has rented where she has something to show him.

DW asks audience if he should go with her. Allows the audience reply to determine his decision, but before they can set off SNOW WHITE takes a shiny red apple from her bag and is about to bite it – DW shouts a warning – too late – she takes a bite and falls to the ground.

DW panics – calls out for help – MOTHER appears with food – she has been following DW because she didn't believe he could cope on his own.

She sees SNOW WHITE on the ground: What have you done, you naughty boy?

She bends over SNOW WHITE – she (SW) needs the kiss of life – MOTHER kisses SNOW WHITE who recovers – MOTHER says you need to come home with me and leave DW to go off to London – they leave – DW asks audience should I go or should I stay at home – audience decides.

Scene 6

Cast come back on in groups:

> OGRE and JACK sheepishly holding hands
> WITCH and RRH
> GOLDILOCKS and ALADDIN
> CINDERELLA and SLEEPING BEAUTY
> DW, MOTHER and SNOW WHITE

Possible themes to explore

- The different stories and endings for well-known pantomime characters
- The plight of young carers
- Nature v nurture in character formation
- The refugee situation
- Traditional pantomime forms – 'he's behind you', for example
- The Royal family
- Press intrusion and privacy.

Staging

Props: three chairs with a throw to create a bench; JACK's food; the stolen cutlery from the Three Bears' house

4. Finding Cinderella

This was created for a luncheon club performance. However, the audience weren't really up to being as involved as we had planned. They had come to be entertained rather than being part of the performance.

Cast

There were two CO-HOSTS

Then there were 3 male actors and 6 female actors available from the company, which determined the number of roles in the pantomime.

Scene 1

CO-HOSTS come on stage and introduce the idea of the play. The audience will help in choosing a Cinderella and two Ugly Sisters for a performance of Cinderella. The actors will be those auditioning but we need your help in getting them made up for an audition to see who will get the parts. You as the audience will also have a vote as to who is successful.

CO-HOSTS assemble the cast who each step forward, introduce themselves, and select 2 or 3 members of the audience to help with getting them ready for the audition.

Each of the cast has a back story so, in addition to their interaction with the audience, there are interactions between the actors. For example:

- *One female actor was a single mother who had come with her baby (a doll) which she left with a member of the audience;*
- *Another had been sent by the job centre;*

- *As in good pantomime tradition, the men were competing for the role of one of the Ugly Sisters while the women were competing for the role of Cinderella.*

Scene 2

Simultaneous short scenes taking place as the sub-groups (one actor plus audience members) help their character get ready using make up and costumes.

Scene 3

CO-HOSTS tell the audience that there are going to be three audition scenes. In each case there will be two Cinderellas and one Ugly Sister. Each time you, the audience, will have to decide which Cinderella is best and at the end of the three scenes which male actor playing an Ugly Sister should be voted off. The voting will be by applause.

The three scenes, reflecting the story, were:

a) The ugly sister and two of the Cinderellas getting ready for the ball. The scene was repeated twice – each Cinderella acted in turn with the Ugly Sister. The audience then voted as to which Cinderella should be sent home. There was an opportunity for interplay in between the actors playing the different roles.
b) The characters receiving the letter saying the prince was coming to see whose foot fitted the slipper – same format
c) The characters trying on the slipper – same format.

Scene 4

The scenes are played out. At the end, there are three candidates to be Cinderella and three Ugly sisters.

The audience are asked to vote off one of the Ugly Sisters, given that two need to be retained for the pantomime, which they do.

We rigged the situation so there didn't need to be a vote for the role of Cinderella as the actor with the baby had to go and feed it and the actor from the Job Centre needed to be back for an interview so it left one winner by default.

All on stage for a final bow.

Possible themes to explore

Because the cast are free to create their own back stories it becomes possible to look at many different issues. In this play among the themes we explored were the plight of the single mother, unemployment and friendship rivalries.

Staging

When we put on the play, we were working on the assumption that, as this audience group had actively participated in a previous show, they would be up for doing it again. Our learning was that this play needed a good warm-up, both before the event and at the beginning. Alternatively, we could have done the dressing up before the show and missed out Scene 2.

The structure of the play was largely determined by the size of the cast.

Props: lots of make-up and dressing-up clothes.

The play also needed a performance space where sub-groups could easily be formed and with sufficient space for the make-up activity to take place.

5. The Women's Institute Pantomime

First performed in December 2013 at the Packhorse Gallery in Huddersfield.

Synopsis

The local Women's Institute decides to put on a panto to raise money for the elderly. The play never gets beyond the first rehearsal.

Cast

Women

JO is married to ANDREW. She is bossy. She is MALCOLM's constituency agent. She thinks MALCOLM is wonderful. She sees a lot of him at weekends and sometimes goes down to London with him. Agrees with him politically. She also has a part-time job as a P.A. She is jealous of ANDREW being retired. In the play, she persuades her husband and the W.I. that he, ANDREW, should direct the panto.

JANICE lives on her own. She has had a lot of directing experience but is continually ignored by other W.I. members, except for LUCY. JANICE has written the panto script.

CANDICE is married to a successful local butcher and is now better off than her former friend, BELINDA. In her eyes, BELINDA was a snob at school who now has a chip on her shoulder because she has gone down in the world. Also, she believes BELINDA tried to pinch her then boyfriend, now husband, ANDREW when they were all at school together. She has five children.

JACKIE is friendly with DEIDRE from college days. When younger, they had good times together including a wild trip to New York. She was going to be a teacher but left before the end of the course to set up in business with her husband, Phillip, who left her for a younger woman. She is now somewhat sarcastic but believes life begins at 40. Has a p/t job at Waitrose and a daughter who lives down south but has no children. Tries unsuccessfully to get DEIDRE to still do things with her. JACKIE has internet dates that DEIDRE disapproves of.

LUCY is a timid woman who is married to MALCOLM. She looks after her ageing father, KEITH, who has come to live with her and MALCOLM after his wife died. She is suspicious of the amount of time MALCOLM spends with JO. She used to be a medical secretary but gave up work when MALCOLM entered politics. Thinks ANDREW will be a great director. Her hobbies are sewing, writing short stories, gardening and making covers for jam pots.

DEIDRE is the chairperson of the W.I.. She is also chair of the magistrates' bench. She is friendly with JACKIE, though they spar a lot. JACKIE doesn't understand how busy she is and also there are limits to what she can do given her positions. Thinks JACKIE is playing with fire with her internet dating. Her husband was a banker but died quite young. She has twin boys at Oxbridge and struggles to support them financially.

BELINDA is married to PAUL, who is ill. They have separate bedrooms because of this, but have fallen foul of the bedroom tax and their home support care has been cut. She now lives on benefits in a council house. Believes CANDICE stole her future husband. She is a committed vegan though PAUL isn't. She can't work because she needs to look after PAUL. Had a good start in life but her father got into trouble with the bank and the banks foreclosed his business. She remains angry with CANDICE and her fur coats.

Men

ANDREW– JO's husband. They have been married for 30 years. He is retired. He used to work for the Ministry of Agriculture, in charge of the depletion of fish stocks. He spends his days at home reading The Stage paper and imagines himself to be a revolutionary theatre director whom the world has been waiting for. Has never in reality acted or directed any play. He is suspicious of MALCOLM because of the time he spends with JO. When the idea of the pantomime is mooted, he has the idea of doing it as an adult production in the round with the cast all in black in semi-darkness.

MALCOLM – LUCY's husband. They met at a local political party 'do'. They don't have children. He is a local Tory M.P., who joined the Conservatives while at university. He is persuaded to help with the panto because it will be good for his image with elections coming up. He fiddles his expenses, claiming the rehearsals are political meetings. He is a director of off-shore tax avoidance companies. He is home most weekends now, given that elections are coming.

PAUL is BELINDA's ill husband.

KEITH is LUCY's father. He is a bit hard of hearing. He pays a nominal £10 a week rent which he thinks makes an important contribution to household expenses. Sees MALCOLM as a visitor to the house he and LUCY share.

Scenes

Scene 1

CANDICE is on stage alone, wearing a fur. BELINDA comes on – sees the fur coat which starts off their quarrel. (During this interchange, they need to establish this is a meeting of the W.I.)

They are interrupted by JO coming on, talking about ANDREW – she is tired of him being at home doing nothing – and about MALCOLM, establishing him as the local M.P. and she as his local agent.

JANICE comes on – is ignored by everyone (JANICE is talked over by everyone except LUCY)

LUCY comes in – acknowledges JANICE – talks about MALCOLM coming home more often and about KEITH and having two men in the house now.

CANDICE & BELINDA continue their argument

DEIDRE & JACKIE arrive – establish DEIDRE as chair. DEIDRE apologises for being late because of JACKIE

Seating places: JO, BELINDA, DEIDRE, CANDICE, LUCY, JANICE, JACKIE

Discussion about use of word 'chairman' – alternative words – 'person', 'chair' but what about words like 'manhole'

Agenda discussion – fund raising

Someone suggests flower arranging

JACKIE suggests speed dating – sets of argument between DEIDRE & JACKIE

JO tells DEIDRE they are drifting off the topic – suggests a dance. This reignites the quarrel between BELINDA and CANDICE over the school dance where it is alleged that BELINDA tried to pinch CANDICE's boyfriend. JO interrupts the quarrel to say they shouldn't argue at a meeting. DEIDRE gets angry with JO because she is the chair and it's her role to keep order.

Someone suggests an auction. Discussion about possible items. Then someone suggests a pantomime.

JANICE tries to say she has written one but is ignored at first until LUCY persuades people to hear her. They agree to the pantomime and move onto a discussion as to who should direct. JO says it should be ANDREW. LUCY says JANICE should, but after a discussion it is agreed that, given there is an all-female cast, maybe they should have a male director.

Everyone leaves at the end except for JO and LUCY. JO says they should get together as a foursome again. LUCY says it's my turn to host.

Scene 2

LUCY's house, post-dinner.

LUCY is off stage making coffee. JO tells ANDREW he should have decaff. MALCOLM offers everyone brandy. There is a discussion as to whether JO or ANDREW is driving home, and therefore who shouldn't drink any more.

MALCOLM & JO finish off a conversation they have been having over dinner about constituency work.

LUCY suggests to JO she should have a part in the panto.

JO realizes she has forgotten to tell ANDREW about his proposed role as director. She does so now. ANDREW starts to fantasize about what he might do.

MALCOLM and ANDREW have a bit of a disagreement – MALCOLM's attitude is both patronising and dismissive of ANDREW.

JO suggests to MALCOLM he could get involved – it would be good for his local image. MALCOLM says he could give a speech at the beginning. JO agreeing puts her hand on MALCOLM's hand and uses word 'darling'. LUCY notices and asks MALCOLM, angrily, to give her a hand in the kitchen. They quarrel off-stage to ANDREW and JO's discomfiture. MALCOLM and LUCY reappear.

KEITH comes in, in his night clothes and offers his £10 rent money. MALCOLM is horrified that this is happening in front of guests. Tries to say it's all a bit of a joke. He didn't realize that KEITH was paying it each week while he was in London.

KEITH asks if he could stay and have a drink too as it's nice and warm down here. MALCOLM goes to get him a drink. JO talks to KEITH and finds he has eaten on his own upstairs. She is scandalised by the fact that he pays rent (even though KEITH is happy to do so because he feels he is making a contribution to the household and LUCY recognizes this).

ANDREW says they should go. He wants to get away from an embarrassing scene. JO says 'good night darling' to MALCOLM.

LUCY says they can see themselves out. ANDREW and JO leave, with ANDREW talking about the exploitation he has witnessed.

LUCY and MALCOLM continue arguing about JO's use of 'darling'. MALCOLM leaves in a huff.

LUCY and KEITH talk for a bit then she helps him up to bed.

Scene 3

Casting at the W.I. meeting for five roles:

    Little Red Riding Hood

    Her Mother

    Grandmother,

    Wolf and Woodcutter

There are five possible actors: DEIDRE, JACKIE, BELINDA, CANDICE, JANICE.

LUCY is doing costumes. JO is front of house.

Cast come in, in same order as before: CANDICE, BELINDA, JO, JANICE, LUCY, DEIDRE, JACKIE.

CANDICE starts on at BELINDA – we've all read JANICE's script and I know what role you should play.

JO comes in building up ANDREW – he isn't there because he is busy building a model set in the attic.

JANICE is ignored.

DEIDRE blames JACKIE for causing her to be late

Arguments as to who should play what role.

BELINDA thinks CANDICE should play the woodcutter because she is married to a butcher

CANDICE thinks BELINDA would be a good wolf because of her love of animals

DEIDRE thinks JACKIE would be a good wolf because of her taste in men

BELINDA & JACKIE both compete to play Red Riding Hood.

DEIDRE says she will play mum

JACKIE says she already dresses for the part

LUCY suggests JANICE should be able to choose her role and thinks JO would be a good wolf – this carries some of the anger from the dinner.

JANICE goes for the grandma role

DEIDRE ends up as mum

BELINDA gets Red Riding Hood, CANDICE gets the Wolf and JACKIE the Woodcutter, because it enables her to show off her wardrobe.

There are conflicts that can be explored:

- LUCY/JO follows on from the dinner in Scene 2, ending up with an almighty row.
- JO/DEIDRE – about who chairs the meeting
- JO is continually acting as ANDREW's spokesperson – 'I think ANDREW had chosen ... for that role.'
- BELINDA/CANDICE – ongoing
- JACKIE/BELINDA – who is the youngest one to play R/Hood – argument over real ages, dying hair etc.

Scene 4

BELINDA/PAUL at home. PAUL on stage in his dressing gown coughing and spluttering.

BELINDA comes in, angry at CANDICE at what happened at casting, then concern about bedroom tax as they can't afford to pay for their second bedroom.

PAUL suggests downsizing to a one-bedroom place but BELINDA says there aren't any in the village and anyway she doesn't want to sleep with him because of his coughing & spluttering and the time she had to change the sheets. She gets angry at PAUL for their misfortune.

PAUL apologises for getting them into this financial mess but BELINDA is tired of it, feels suicidal and goes off to bed.

PAUL staggers off after her.

Scene 5: The Rehearsal

ANDREW and JO on stage, ANDREW fussing, JO saying it will be alright. JO leaves.

CANDICE & BELINDA enter – ANDREW tries to sort out what roles they have and gets it wrong.

LUCY comes bringing KEITH with her saying that he can sit and watch the rehearsal. LUCY wants to talk to ANDREW about what happened at the dinner while ANDREW only wants to talk about the play.

JO comes in with MALCOLM. Conflicts – MALCOLM / BELINDA re bedroom tax & LUCY / JO re JO being with MALCOLM again.

JANICE comes on and wants to talk to ANDREW about some changes he has made but he dismisses them and her. LUCY tries to intervene to support JANICE but is unsuccessful.

DEIDRE and JACKIE come in, apologizing yet again for JACKIE holding her up. JACKIE has come in, in a costume for the Woodcutter which ANDREW immediately says is wrong and not his idea of what should happen.

ANDREW then tries to persuade them of his idea of what should happen and tries to get them to start doing as he says – rebellion slowly grows. The women (except for JO and LUCY) start to support each other. JO is caught in the middle, wanting to support her husband but realizing that the group is right and he is hopeless. JO argues they should give ANDREW more time and appeals to

MALCOLM to help her cause. MALCOLM realizes this is turning into a catastrophe that he doesn't want anything to do with and he leaves. He tries to take KEITH and LUCY with him but she and KEITH want to stay – LUCY stops being the doormat in their relationship and MALCOLM leaves asking JO to come with him so that they can talk work some more. JO asks ANDREW if she is needed but ANDREW is too busy trying to save his director role. JO reluctantly follows MALCOLM off

LUCY emerges as the strong one pushing JANICE's case forward. The rest slowly recognize that she could save the day. They turn to JANICE who does so – she starts saying assertively what will happen – suggests a break as its time for lunch – curtain

Possible themes to explore

- As in any pantomime – political issues of the day
- Retirement
- Dating problems in middle age
- Life's unrealistic dreams
- Drink driving
- Married men's behaviour
- The lasting power of childhood grievances

Staging

In the performances, we gave JANICE the freedom to end it as she chose. She could either 'save the day' or refuse to do so. The rest of the cast wouldn't know which option she would choose.

The set was simply a table and chairs which could be rearranged to either be the W.I. meeting room or a living/dining room.

SECTION 3: Dementia and Ageing

1. Five Short Plays:

    i.   Growing Old Ain't Easy

    ii.   Sexual Rights

    iii.   Loneliness

    iv.   Oh No She Won't

    v.   Retired

2. Seeking Joan

3. Sketches

1. Five Short Plays

These plays are all to do with dementia and ageing. Two of them – *Growing Old Ain't Easy* and *Oh No She Won't* – were commissioned by Kirklees Council and can be seen on their website as well as on our Facebook page. As you will see on the videos, these scripts were used only as a base from which the actors could improvise.

i. Growing Old Ain't Easy

This play was retitled 'Little Things make a Difference' for the Kirklees video performance.

A conversation between a mother (M) and a daughter (D).

D: How are you feeling today?

M: Where am I?

D: Here, home with me.

M: How long have I been here?

D: About a couple of months now.

M: Am I happy?

D: I don't hear you complaining.

M: What day is it?

D: Saturday.

M: I got married on a Saturday. I wore a white address.

D: You mean dress

M: That's what I said. Now, where was I?

D: You were telling me about getting married.

M: Who did I get married to? I can't remember.

D: Phil, your husband, my father.

M: I remember an Alfred.

D: That was your father.

M: Was I married to him?

D: No, Phil was your husband.

M: What day is it?

D: Saturday.

M: I got married on a Saturday.

D: What would you like to wear today?

M: Wear my red dress.

D: It's in the wash.

M: I want my red dress.

D: Janice is coming today.

M: Who is Janet? I don't know any Janet.

D: Janice, she's your grand-daughter.

M: Is she related to you?

D: She's my daughter.

M: Is today Monday?

D: No Saturday.

M: I got married on a Saturday.

D: I know, mum.

M: Have I told you?

D: Once or twice.

M: That's okay then.

D:	How about getting up?

M:	Only if I can wear my red dress.

D:	It's in the wash.

M:	Well, I won't get up then.

D:	Don't you want your breakfast.

M:	I'll have a rasher of toast and a fried egg.

D:	That's bacon, egg and toast.

M:	That's what I said. What day is it?

D:	Saturday.

M:	Am I going to the day centre today?

D:	Not on Saturday.

M:	I got married on a Saturday.

D:	Do you want to look at some photos after breakfast?

M:	They make me sad. I was pretty once.

D:	You still are.

M:	No one wants me anymore.

D:	I do mum.

M:	There's no one anymore.

D:	There's me, mum.

M:	You are just my daughter.

D:	There is me here, mum.

M:	I'm all alone. I never amounted to much. Your dad …

D:	I don't want to hear the story about dad again.

M: He did what he wanted. Never asked me. Men are like that. I warned you, didn't I? Better to have nothing to do with them than put up with their filthy habits.

D: You are making yourself upset again.

M: What day is it.?

D: Shall we have breakfast?

M: Is it that time already? I will have porridge.

D: It's a warm summer day. How about some bacon, eggs and toast?

M: That would be nice, dear. Did you ever get married?

D: You know I did, mum, to Derek and then he left me for a younger version.

M: I'm positive he didn't mean to.

D: I don't think there was much doubt about it.

M: I was married once, on a Saturday. What happened to him?

D: He fell ill and then he passed away.

M: Where to, where did he go to? Why didn't anyone tell me? Can we go and see him?

D: Mum, he died.

M: Why, didn't you say so?

D: Time to get up.

M: I think I will stay in bed today. I feel tired.

D: You need to get up for a bit, otherwise you will get more bed sores.

M: Later, I'm just going to have a little sleep.

D: Night, mum.

M: Night, dear, don't let the bed bugs bite. Do you know when we were little we had bed bugs, little red bites, you scratched all day.

D: There are none here.

M: Are you sure?

D: Yes.

M: You are a good daughter.

D: Sometimes.

M: What was that?

D: Nothing, mum – go to sleep now.

M: Sing to me.

D: Oh mum!

M: Please, just a little song.

D: *(singing)* Rock-a-bye baby in the tree tops, when the wind blows the cradle will rock … night, mum.

ii. Sexual rights

This is a discussion between a care worker (W) and a resident (R) in a residential home

W: Please turn that off.

R: Why?

W: It's offensive.

R: It's my room. I can watch what I like on my computer.

W: Not if it offends someone else.

R: Then don't look.

W: That's not the point.

R: You can't dictate what I watch. That's censorship.

W: This is a residential home.

R: This is my room.

W: But staff need to come in. They don't want to see that.

R: They should knock first.

W: Anyway, why do you want to watch stuff like that at your age?

R: Just because you are 80, it doesn't mean you don't have sexual urges.

W: It's not proper at your age.

R: You mean at any age.

W: I didn't say that.

R: How else can I get satisfaction at my age? None of the ladies here seem to be interested and even if they were it would be frowned upon.

W: We have to look after the interests of all the residents.

R: If I had a collection of Playboy hidden under the mattress then that would be okay?

W: It wouldn't be as bad. It's just pictures – but what you are looking at is people actually doing it.

R: So how do you think we all got here?

W: There's a time and place for everything.

R: And this is my time and place.

W: You know the rules – no offensive behaviour.

R: But if I'm here on my own, whom am I offending?

W: What would happen if your daughter found out?

R: She would be disgusted probably.

W: So, isn't that a good reason to stop?

R: But all children have difficulty coping with the idea that their parents have a sexual life.

W: I think your daughter should know. It's not appropriate behaviour.

R: That would be a breach of contract.

W: It is your daughter who pays your fees.

R: That still doesn't give you the right to tell her things that are private.

W: It can't be that private if I found you doing this.

R: It was just because I didn't hear you knock. My hearing isn't what it was.

W: I am shocked and upset by what I saw.

R: I can't be responsible for your sensibilities.

W: Don't you ever think about the poor women who are forced to take part in what you are watching?

R: There are programmes on the internet where people film themselves having sex and then put it on the internet themselves.

W: I don't believe that.

R: Whether you believe it or not, it's true. Some people get turned on by knowing other people are watching and everyone to quote Andy Warhol deserves their 15 minutes of fame.

W: Well, I don't and anyway sex and all of that is something that should be private .. between a man and a woman ...

R: Or between a man and a man and a ...

W: Don't even go there.

R: I have my rights as a resident and a citizen.

W: And I have rights as a worker and that includes not being subjected to things that are offensive.

R: Why is people having sex offensive?

W: Because it's not something we thrust in each other's faces. I mean what would your wife have said if she had found you doing this.?

R: She did.

W: And?

R: We had an almighty row.

W: So you should have learnt your lesson.

R: What lesson?

W: That women aren't turned on by pornography – that they feel lessened by it.

R: That's very much what she said.

W: So

R: But she's not here anymore and I'm still a sexual being. Anyway, you would be horrified if I started to grope the staff – I wouldn't last long then.

W: Dead right.

R: And if phoned up one of those numbers where you can have someone come and give you a so-called massage at home you wouldn't be any happier.

W: You know our rules concerning guests.

R: But I read recently where disabled young people were helped with the use of sexual surrogates.

W: It's not the same and anyway I wouldn't go along with that.

R: What's not the same?

W: They weren't old.

R: So it's my age that is at the root of it?

W: That. My husband and I have put all of that behind us.

R: That's your choice.

W: It's what most people of our age do and particularly when they get to be as old as you are.

R: How do you know? I bet that it's not something you talk about with your friends.

W: There's no need to.

R: So how do you know?

W: Just grow up.

R: I'm 80 years old. How much more grown up can I become?

W: That's not what I meant and you know it.

R: Suppose I said I would only look at it late at night?

W: You mean when everyone is back in their rooms in the evening?

R: Yes.

W: But I still feel that it is not appropriate to have that stuff on view anytime.

R: Pornography is one of the most accessed subjects on the internet.

W: That doesn't make it right.

R: But it's not unusual. It's what guys and some women do when they are not getting it in real life and that's my situation. You should be thankful that I have this relief.

W: I just wish that I had never seen this in the first place. It's not an image I want to carry around with me. I feel nauseated. Aren't you embarrassed?

R: A little at being caught, but not otherwise.

W: Aren't you worried about getting addicted?

R: There are worse fates at my age. Anyway, it's one of the few things not dragging my health down.

W: It's not only your physical health I was thinking of.

R: It's a bit too late to be worried about that now.

W: So no more?

R: Definitely not while you're on duty.

iii. Loneliness

A two-hander between a care worker (H) and a housebound individual (S).

S: I haven't seen you before.

H: No, I'm just filling in.

S: Where were you born?

H: I was just born three streets from here.

S: Oh

H: No, it's just your accent is a bit unusual.

H: People get used to it.

S: Could you put my shopping away.

H: I've done what I'm paid for.

S: Please wait a bit.

H: I can't, I've got to be at my next appointment in 10 minutes.

S: So, what am I going to do for the rest of the day?

H: What do you normally do?

S: I sit at the window and watch the world go by.

H: You've got the T.V.

S: How many times can you watch programmes about houses you can't afford or holidays you can't go on or young people with the whole of their life before them, before you go mad?

H: You have the paper delivered.

S: It's always bad news, wars, economic crises – why do I want to read about that? I know the world is going to the dogs. It's true what they say. You come into this world alone and you leave it alone.

H: Unless you're a twin.

S: What's the point?

H: Doesn't anyone call?

S: They have either died or gone away.

H: No relatives?

S: A son in Australia, but he has children and can't get away.

H: Your grandchildren?

S: I've only seen them once. When my wife/husband was still alive, five years ago we went and visited them. We always dreamed we would grow old surrounded by children and grandchildren. Funny how life turns out. Just you on your own as everything crumbles around you.

H: You could always see them on the internet.

S: It's not the same and anyway I'm too old to learn all that malarkey.

H: Life can't be all bad?

S: When you have pills for this and pills for that and a pain in my shoulder which won't go away and a rickety knee which they won't do anything about and makes it painful to walk – it's not a great life.

H: You know they are going to reduce the number of times I can come unless you can pay for me – it's the cutbacks.

S: I can barely get by on my pension. Where would I have the money to pay for you?

H: There's some system where the council gives you money to employ people. Perhaps you could qualify for that?

S: I bet that's likely and who would help me manage something like that. Mary down the street had someone in to mend her shower and they swindled her of over £1,000. You can't trust anyone anymore. It's all too much for me. I need things to be as simple as possible. All these choices make the world too confusing and you never know what's the best deal.

H: Look, I must go.

S: Please help me into that chair over by the window.

H: Okay … what's going on here? You're wet.

S: Please help me.

H: I can't, it's not part of my job description.

S: I have to stay in my soiled clothes?

H: What would you do if I wasn't here?

S: Please, please, just this once. I can't bear the loneliness, it's degrading to be reduced to this, having to beg …what world have we come to when people have to sit in their piss-stained clothes watching from the windows, screaming si-

lently at the world to notice … have some humanity woman.

H: I must go, I'm late, it's not part of my job to change you, I'm sorry, you'll just have to manage. I'll see you on Friday.

S: Gone, gone, well at least I'm warm and wet. It will be pads next, togged up in nappies, back to being a baby – like they say from cradle to grave and back again … wonder what I'll be in my next life. Knowing my luck, I'll be a plague-carrying rat … oh look, it's that fat lady wobbling down the road … what have I done to deserve this? … I've tried to live a god-fearing life, why, for what purpose and now everything is against me … talking to myself … some psychologist once said to me that if you don't find yourself interesting enough to talk to why should anyone else … oh look, it's her from down the road …wave …no, don't be silly – she won't want to know.

iv. Oh No She Won't

A three-hander between a daughter (D), her husband (H) and her mother (M).

M: I don't want to be a burden.

D: I couldn't put you in a home.

H: She's not going to live with us.

D: She's my mum, she's spent most of her life looking after me; now it's my turn to give back to her.

H: But not at the expense of our relationship.

M: I've had my life, so I don't want you to worry about me.

D: It wouldn't be a worry. You have so much you could offer us. We would always have a baby-sitter on hand..

H: That's fine for now. What about when her condition gets worse.?

D: We can cross that bridge when we get to it.

H: It would probably mean you having to give up the job that you love and our household income would go down. It would be the end of foreign holidays.

D: So we would be helping to save the planet.

H: So anyway where would she sleep? I'm not giving up my office.

D: Why not? It would be the perfect space.

H: No, I need somewhere for me to do my work.

D: Where's my space and what about all those promises that you were not going to bring your work home?

H: You'll be expecting me to do my work at the kitchen table as if I was one of the children doing my homework.

D: Well what do you want me to do? She is mother. We can't just put her out on the street. She's not capable of looking after herself anymore.

H: We could always look for ways of putting in more help.

D: And if she had another fall, left the gas on again or went off wandering once more. She lives too far away for me to pop in and see that she's okay. Anyway, you and the kids are always complaining about our weekends being taken up with going to see her.

H: Perhaps it's time to consider a nursing home.

D: You know how expensive they are and you're always complaining that we're short of money as it is.

H: We could sell her home to pay for it.

D: Have you ever been in one of these homes? They're places for the living dead.

M: What's this talk about selling my place? I don't want to move. I've lived there all my life. It's my home. It's where I was brought up.

D: Wouldn't you like to come and live with us here?

M: I like what I know. I don't want to change at my time of life.

D: But mum I'm worried about you living on your own. Last week you had put your handbag in the fridge and panicked when you couldn't find it. And what if you had another fall?

M: I've got one of those call alarm things.

D: But you never wear it. Yesterday I found it in the fruit bowl.

H: If my office isn't on the table so to speak where would your mum sleep?

D: The boys could always share and bunk up.

M: I wouldn't want to get in their way.

D: You couldn't do that ever mum.

H: *(quietly)* Like heck.

D: What was that?

H: Nothing.

D: You're leaving everything to me as always.

H: She is your mum.

D: And I didn't do anything when your mum was dying?

H: What do you think the boys will make of having to share a room?

D: They love their gran. They'll get used to it.

H: I wouldn't be so sure. They fight enough at the moment. Put them in the same room and it will be bedlam.

D: You would like to see more of your grandsons, wouldn't you mum?

M: I see them the most weekends.

D: But if you lived here you could see them every day.

M: I'm not so sure.

D: Suppose you came to stay here for a week, have a sort of holiday.

H: Hold on, you are jumping to conclusions here. We haven't finished our discussion and you are already trying to get her to move in.

D: Only for a week.

H: Yes, I bet. It will turn into a fait accompli. She'll survive the week and then you will persuade her to stay for another week and before one can say 'Jack Robinson' she'll be firmly ensconced. It's how you operate. It's how you've done things like this in the past.

D: She's coming whether you like it or not.

M: Coming where?

H: Doesn't she get a say? It's only her life we're talking about.

M: I don't like this. Take me home please.

D: Mum, come and stay for a week.

M: I would like that.

D: That's settled then.

H: We'll see.

v. Retired

A dialogue between a physiotherapist (D) and a patient (P).

D: How are you today?

P: Not bad – and you?

D: Can't complain. So how is that shoulder doing? Can you take off your shirt and sit down in that chair and give us a look … how about that?

P: That's okay ..oo!. That hurts, just there.

D: That's the spot.

P: Just around there, it's really sore – what do you think it is?

D: It's most likely a damaged tendon that's giving you the pain.

P: What's caused it?

D: Probably just wear and tear. We'll try a combination of exercise and rest. You're retired, aren't you?

P: No.

D: But I see you're 72 years old.

P: So?

D: So you could probably do with taking it easy now.

P: Why?

D: You've earned it.

P: What do you mean? That having a rest is all that we should aspire to?

D: No, simply if you have worked hard all your life, you are entitled to take things easy.

P: Do my garden, play a round of golf, take a long holiday, that sort of things?

D: Something like that.

P: And throw in a bit of voluntary work, help at the local day centre?

D: Yes.

P: So your advice to political leaders, academics, judges and artists who are in their 70s is that they stop and take up gardening?

D: Of course not.

P: So why is your advice relevant to me?

D: Because you're complaining of things which would benefit from taking it easier.

P: And if I was younger and needing to work?

D: Probably an eight-session programme with lots of home-work.

P: So I'm being treated differently because of my age?

D: Age comes into it, it's what's contributing to the wear and tear.

P: Well I'm going to keep working. I'm off to a conference in America next month. It's ironic, isn't it? In the past, we oldies were a drain on the state to be locked away out of sight and now suddenly we're expected to keep working forever while struggling to keep our house going. In the end, it's all down to money.

D: Give me another look at your back.

P: Why?

D: Did you know you've got a lump in between your shoulder blades?

P: No, how could I see that?

D: Do you know how long you've had it?

P: If I didn't know it was there how would I know how long I've had it?

D: It's probably nothing to worry about but I think you should take yourself off to see your doctor.

P: But you said there was nothing to worry about.

D: You can never be too safe. You can put your shirt back on.

P: Just a moment – you tell me not to worry but bringing this lump I can't see to my attention and then telling me not to worry means that I will now worry about something that wasn't a worry two minutes ago.

D: If I hadn't brought it to your attention then I would have been negligent.

P: It took me two weeks to get the appointment at the doctors which led to the eight-week wait to see you.

D: Is there anything else?

P: You could look at my knee – it's getting painful going up and down stairs.

D: I can't I'm afraid.

P: Why not?

D: The doctor only referred you for your shoulder. Your knee would need a new referral.

P: That's ridiculous – my knee is a problem now.

D: But we only get paid for each episode or problem.

P: So if I want my knee seeing to then I have to go back through the whole system again?

D: You could always go private.

P: That's just they want, isn't it? Run down the NHS so those that can afford it will go private and we'll end up with a two-tier health system.

D: I'm sorry I can't help you.

P: I thought you were meant to treat the whole body, the whole person.

D: That's not the way it works anymore. Each part of our body is a separate cost centre which needs to be charged for. That's how it works now.

P: So I have to limp along for another two months even though I am here now in front of you.

D: My hands are tied. I'm sorry. Look can I at least give you some exercises for your shoulder.

P: Don't bother.

Possible themes to explore

- Aspects of caring for someone with dementia
- Life in a care home
- Sexuality in old age
- Crises in the social care system
- Zero hour contracts
- Ageing society

2. Seeking Joan

This play was a bit different in so far as it was commissioned by Kirklees Dementia Action Alliance, University of Huddersfield Department of Human and Health Sciences, West Yorkshire Police and Kirklees Social Services to help introduce the Herbert Protocol. This was a written document to aid people looking for missing people, especially those with dementia. The play was first performed at the University of Huddersfield on June 22nd 2016. The play became very popular and we performed it for a number of different audiences. It is available to see on YouTube as well as on our Facebook page.

Cast

Joan, who has dementia

Her Son

Her Daughter-in-law (Son's wife) (abbreviated to D-i-L)

Her Granddaughter (abbreviated to GD)

Her Daughter – lives away in London – married – well off

Neighbour

Audience 1&2 – bickering Husband and Wife – they sit in the audience

Scenes

Scene 1

Son's house. D-i-L on stage, worried – Son enters, has been called home from work. He and D-i-L argue.

Son: Where is my mother?

D-i-L: I had to go out – I thought I had locked the door – where could she have gone – I have phoned all her

	usual haunts and walked around the neighbourhood – what should we do –
Son:	*(blaming)* All you have to do is look after her.
D-i-L:	She's your mother – you go out to work all day – I need to have a life too – trying to do my best – I am not appreciated.

The quarrel continues along these lines.

They leave the stage to have a cup of tea.

Joan appears in the audience – wandering, muttering – number 10, Molly

Audience pair comment on the play they are watching:

Audience 1:	Is she ok?
Audience 2:	Don't get involved – perhaps she's drunk.
Audience 1:	We should help.
Audience 2:	Don't you go, you can't have a strange man accosting a lady in the street, not these days.

Neighbour appears – rescues Joan and takes her on the way home – they remain off stage.

On stage, Son and D-i-L reappear, still arguing about who is responsible and what they should do.

Knock on the door and Neighbour and Joan appear.

Home scene – relief – Joan bewildered by the fuss –

Joan:	I only went to visit my friend.

Son goes back to work – Joan and D-i-L go offstage to the kitchen to have a cup of tea.

Audience pair stand up and comment on the play so far, making clear people's different reactions to dementia. They then notice actors coming back and sit down.

Scene 2

A week later – family get together – Joan, Son, her D-i-L and GD, home from University. This is a meeting to decide what needs to be done about Joan. While they are waiting for Joan's Daughter to arrive, there is an argument between Son and D-i-L over Joan's Daughter, who D-i-L thinks should do more to help.

Daughter appears – ignores D-i-L – fusses over Joan. A further argument develops in between Son, D-i-L and Daughter over who is responsible for Joan. Son complaining that his sister is the golden girl who only visits occasionally. Daughter says 'you live closer and your wife doesn't work'. D-i-L says she's got a life too and has her own activities. Discussion as to whether Joan should go into a home – question of who would pay. GD says her gran shouldn't be kept a prisoner.

Joan is present but ignored by all but GD.

Daughter leaves angrily to go to a work meeting – the reason she came up north – Son goes to work – rest leave to have a cuppa.

As actors leave stage, Audience 1&2 stand up again commenting on the scene particularly on whether people with dementia should be in a home.

Scene 3

A month later – only Son, D-i-L and GD are present. Again, they are waiting for Daughter. Son says he has been to talk to a social worker through his doctor – given this Herbert protocol to fill in – tells story of its background – emphasises it stays with the family and other interested people i.e. neighbour should get a copy – they start filling in the form – get to the stage where they need information about where Joan used to live – Daughter arrives – fills in missing information, which highlights origins of number 10 and Molly. They decide to have a cuppa – GD discovers Joan is missing – accusations all around – then Daughter gets into the car to look for her – GD is going to raise alarm on social media – Son and D-i-L start to fill in the part of the form to be completed when someone goes missing – Son's phone rings - Joan has been found in a supermarket, which is one of the advertised safe dementia places.

Son and D-i-L say they will go and pick her up.

Stage now empty.

Audience 1&2 stand up – wife says we'd better go because you will be needing help soon enough. They walk onto the stage and as they do, the rest of the cast comes and joins them and all take a bow.

Possible themes to explore

- The child who lives furthest away and does the least to help with daily activities is often seen in a more positive light than the one who does the daily care
- Cut backs in local health and social care resources – include closures of homes, day centres
- Cost of care – illustrated by how little daughter is prepared to offer son to help look after mum
- Show how looking after someone with dementia creates family tensions.
- Patronising attitudes towards Joan – blaming the victim
- The psychological cost to the carer, who becomes a prisoner
- The Herbert Protocol
- The concept of safe places for people at risk

Staging

The only props used were five chairs with a throw over two chairs making a couch.

The script was adjusted for each performance. In one case, there was no audience as we were short of actors. On another occasion, the play started with the first action being Audience 1&2 arriving after the lights had gone down, bickering. On another occasion, when the play was put on for a teenage audience, we changed

Scene 3, creating instead an extended dialogue between GD and D-i-L where GD could voice her fears about her gran.

At other performances, we alternated actors playing the different roles. This was usually necessitated by who was available but served to keep performances fresh and actors on their toes.

We also created a shorter version by combining Scenes 2 & 3 when the play was put on at conferences, so that it could be used as an interlude between different speakers.

3. Sketches

This shows the structure of a typical performance geared for a care home audience – a series of 'variety' type Acts, built around cast members' skills.

Cast

Ralph – Host

Paul

Jackie

Joe

Carly, Alec & Mike

Babs

Liz & Colin

Scenes

Ralph, as Host, introduces each Act to the care home residents.

Paul – as a 'difficult' member of the cast, interrupts after each Act saying 'I don't want to be here. I just want to go home'.

Act 1 – Jackie, introduced by Ralph, sings – 'My Old Man'

Paul intervenes – told to sit down.

Act 2 – Joe, introduced by Ralph, sings the 'Bumble Bee' song

Paul intervenes – told to sit down.

Act 3 – introduced by Ralph – Carly, Alec and Mike do an act where Carly asks the audience to help her choose between the two men who want to marry her – sets them a competition – who can sing the best song, who has the greatest knobbly knees and who can give the best reason why she should choose them. Each time, after both contestants have had a go, she gets the audience to choose who did best.

Act 4 – Babs, after Ralph's introduction, tells a story about why people can't visit on different days of the week.

Paul intervenes – told to sit down again.

Act 5 – Ralph introduces Liz and Colin, who do an act where he plays a traditional husband, coming home from work and expecting his wife, Liz, to have prepared his dinner. Liz complains to the audience about how terrible it is to live with such a husband, encouraging audience involvement.

Paul then sings 'I just want to go home' – rest of the cast join in.

Possible themes to explore

We do quite a lot of work in care homes – our main aim each time is to entertain. We try to maximise audience involvement, using stories plus songs and props which the audience can recognize from earlier times in their lives.

Staging

We normally find ourselves working in a small space with the audience in a variety of chairs, some alert and some dozing. We try to keep those who are awake involved and to awaken those who are cat-napping. We usually have one or two members of staff in the room with us.

The advantage we have is that some of our cast will be the same age as many in the audience and can relate, from firsthand experience, to many of the life experiences the audience will have known.

SECTION 4: One-off Plays

1. The Time Keepers

2. Cleopatra's Nightclub

3. The Old Biddies

4. The Colander Girls

1. The Time Keepers

Cast

The Family:

    Father

    Mother

    Older Daughter – 23, still living at home (OD)

    Teenage Daughter (TD)

The Time Keepers

    Kat – Team Leader

    July

    Paul

    Dot

    Chrissy – a new member

    Jody – a problem member, as she can't keep to time

Scenes

Scene One

Typical family breakfast scene. There is a clock but it's not working – time is standing still.

July, a Time Keeper, is on the edge of the stage, out of sight of the family members, with a stopwatch clocking up all the activities.

Father is busy, wanting to get off to work, says he lost time yesterday because he got caught up in a traffic jam and arrived late for a meeting.

OD says I can't find my car keys – 'I'm always wasting time looking for things.'

TD is in bed, refusing to get up.

Mother: I won't have time to do everything that I need to do today.

She asks her husband if he can take TD to the school play in the evening.

Father: I can't, I have too much work to do.

Mother: We never have any time together anymore.

Father: We watched TV together last night.

Mother: Sitting on separate sofas.

Father: But in the same space.

Mother: I mean quality time.

Father: What about the new dishwasher?

Mother: You're right, that should help save a bit of time.

Father: I need to be off.

He grabs a briefcase and leaves, as does OD, who has now found her keys.

TD comes down in her pyjamas.

Mother: You'll be late for school. Have you done your homework?

TD: I didn't have time.

Mother: What about last night?

TD: I had to have a bath and wash my hair.

Mother: Well, go and get into your school uniform and then come back down and grab a bite to eat.

TD: I won't have time for breakfast. I'll get something at the shop.

Mother: " But …

TD has left. Mother grabs up empty dishes and also leaves.

Scene Two

A meeting of the Time Keepers. Kat, Paul, July, Dot and Chrissy are present.

Kat calls the meeting to order and introduces Chrissy as a new member joining the team. She explains the role and purpose of the Time Keepers to Chrissy. Their job is to help families save time, which is a precious resource.

Jody comes in after the meeting has started and gets a ticking off from Kat.

Paul is an old fashioned male factory worker who thinks women are not up to the job. Finds that time drags now that he is older. Thinks, therefore, that if people lived more boring lives then they would feel they were living longer.

July is an ex-time and motion worker, who is reporting back on the family. She reports that TD took 75 minutes to have a bath. There is a discussion about how long a bath should take.

Then July reports about Father losing time in a traffic jam. Discussion as to whether it's his fault – should have used a GPS – also, he used his toilet time to read a magazine – Kat notes that a typical man over his lifetime spends the equivalent of five months sitting on the toilet reading.

Paul: And what do we get – piles!

Kat: Don't talk to me about piles.

Kat wonders whether Father is spending too long shaving – if it takes him 15 minutes a day then over his lifetime he will have spent 3 months just shaving.

General discussion about time – possible points:

  'prisoners serving time'

  'time waits for no man'

Kat decides they need to set up a meeting to help this family save time.

People leave. Kat asks July to stay behind – she needs her advice. The Government, due to the economic crisis, needs to raise money. Is thinking of privatising time. They've privatised water, gas and electricity and are on the way to privatising health so why not time? The minister wants ideas as to how they might do this.

They have a serious discussion – for example:

- they could bundle it up and sell it on ebay;
- the unemployed could sell their spare time, gaining an income and helping the economy to grow. The government could then tax their income to raise more revenue;
- the unemployed could just stay in bed, stop the clocks in their houses so time would stand still and therefore not be wasted;
- alternatively, people could deposit time in a time bank, though the bank would have to be careful not to lend out too much time or the country would run out of time and hence there would be another crisis.

They leave to have a cup of tea.

Scene three

In the family house. Paul and Mother onstage

Paul: What's your problem?

Mother: I've started to save some time now but how do I keep it? If I have time I don't need, can I give it to one of my daughters because they never have enough time?

Session continues along these lines. Paul starts off confident but as the Mother asks him questions he becomes flustered, she gets the upper hand and he looks for a way out.

Paul leaves.

Husband arrives. They have a short discussion as to how the session went. Mother leaves to take the dog for a walk.

Husband sits waiting. Looking at his watch.

Jody arrives, apologises for being late but she lost the time.

Husband: How can you lose time? Did you go back and look for it?

Jody: *(flustered)* I'm here now.

Husband: But you're late, we've both lost time.

Jody: Shall we at least look for the time you've lost?

Husband: No, then we'll lose more time looking for the time we've already lost.

Jody: Well, I need to go and retrace my path to see if I can find my lost time.

She leaves.

Wife comes back in. They discuss how the husband's session went. Husband concludes it was a waste of time.

OD arrives for her session.

Husband and wife leave.

Dot arrives. Dot gives OD some straightforward advice about how to find lost things.

Daughter talks about how every minute is monitored at work now. and they even check out if you stop to talk to another employee. Your computer measures everything you do. All breaks are timed.

Dot tries to argue that this is a good thing as time is precious.

Daughter disagrees, saying her employer doesn't have the right to own every minute of her time. It's exploitation.

Dot says that's the way the world is going and concludes by saying she'd like to meet up after work to find a quieter time to continue the talk.

OD: Is that allowed?

Dot: Yes, if we don't have to work overtime.

OD: How can something be overtime. Time only happens once.

They leave still talking.

TD comes in with Chrissy. Chrissy is apologising, saying she's new to the job.

TD: Well, you won't be much use to me then.

Chrissy tries to help her by talking about the amount of time she is wasting in bed, in the bath etc. but TD says it's her time to do what she wants with.

Chrissy gives up and leaves. Teenager also goes.

Scene four

Family house. OD and Mother present.

Mother goes to a suitcase and asks OD to guess what is in it. OD tries but can't guess.

Mother: I've saved some time, today. Do you want it?

OD: I could do with some. I'm going out in half-an-hour and I don't have time to wash my hair first. Where is your saved time?

Mother: It's in the suitcase. I have it locked away.

She looks for the key but can't find it.

Mother: I know I put it somewhere. If you can find it, you can have some of my time. I think I might have left it upstairs."

OD goes off. TD comes in.

Mother: You need to go and finish your homework.

TD: There's not enough time.

Mother retells suitcase story.

Mother: You can have some of it, if you don't waste it. Your sister is looking for the key. If you help her find it you can have some.

TD leaves. Father comes in.

Mother: You're home early.

Father: Yes, I took a short cut and saved fifteen minutes.

A pause while they listen to the two daughters off stage arguing about where the key might be and who will have most right to Mother's time.

Mother: *(to Father)* Give them some time. They'll sort it out. They can always have the 20 minutes you've just saved.

Father: But that was for us.

Argument offstage continues.

Mother: I have had enough. Your turn to go and sort it out.

Father leaves.

Mother pulls out the key from under her sweater, unlocks the suitcase and takes out a Time Out magazine, puts her feet up and says:

Mother: This is my time.

Possible themes to explore

- Privatisation
- Employers monitoring of employees' time at work
- What lies behind sayings about 'time'.

Staging

Basic one set of a table and chair arranged either as a family room or a meeting room

Props: suitcase, clock, briefcase, key, Time Out magazine

2. Cleopatra's Nightclub

Audience are seated around small tables as in a night club.

Cast

Jackie and Josie –two waitresses

Judy – bar manager

Paul, – nightclub owner

Andrew – local councilor and customer

Matthew – local bank manager and customer

Diana – Andrew's wife

Kim – Andrew and Diana's daughter

Carol – an experienced pole-dancer

Scenes

1. Josie and Joan come in and start cleaning tables, gossiping, interacting with the audience – offering to get drinks. Judy is sitting at a table on her own, with papers around her, working away.

2. Kim and Diana peer in. Diana needs a pee. Kim (who is a worldly-wise 21-year old) explains to her mum that it will be ok for her to go and use the toilet. While Diana enters, and goes straight across the stage to the toilet, Kim approaches Judy and asks if they have any jobs going, as she is a university graduate who can't find a job. Judy asks her to come back later. Diana comes back complaining about the state of the toilets and demands they leave. Kim and Diana leave.

3. Paul comes in and sits with Judy. He complains about hard times, business rates going up etc. They need to bring in more customers – they need more pole dancers. Paul says he has one,

Carol, at another of his establishments who could come and do a lunchtime slot. Paul leaves speaking on his mobile.

4. Josie and Jackie continue to clean tables – they then start to play around with the pole. Paul comes back in – sees them and asks if one of them would be interested in doing a pole-dancing slot. Josie is possibly interested.

5. Andrew enters – goes and sits with Judy and they converse. It becomes clear he is a local councillor who is well known there. Paul comes in and joins them and tries to ensure that his licence will be renewed.

6. Carol enters – Paul greets her – asks her to show Josie some basic moves. Andrew and Paul move to a new table to watch this. Andrew then asks Jackie to go and get him and Paul a sandwich. Jackie leaves. Josie and Carol finish their moves. They sit and talk in the background.

7. Jackie re-enters with sandwiches at the same time as Matthew comes in. He joins Andrew & Paul and is clearly known to them. They start talking about the club – Matthew is threatening to call in the loan as headquarters are getting tough with outstanding loans.

8. Paul gets up and goes over to Carol and Josie and asks if one of them will put on a show for the customers. Josie was only toying with the idea and when Carol shows her the costume she would have to wear, Josie refuses and walks out. Paul goes back to Andrew and Matthew.

9. Kim comes back in to talk to Judy about a job. Judy says there is only a vacancy for a pole dancer, suggests she talks to Carol. Kim, still not having seen Andrew, goes over to Carol. Judy goes to Paul and says she thinks she has a possible new dancer. Paul goes over to Carol and Kim and is quite creepy.

11. Andrew notices what is happening and that it is Kim, his daughter who is thinking of being a pole dancer. Confrontation between the two with Kim wanting to know what her dad is doing in a place like this. Diana comes back in while this is going on as

she has finished shopping and was looking everywhere for Kim. She is horrified both by Kim wanting a job and her husband being here. They leave still arguing.

12. Matthew realises this is not doing his reputation any good and gets up to leave, with Paul following, pleading for more time to repay the loan.

13. Jackie, Judy and Carol sitting at a table, wondering whether they will still have a job, how demeaning this work is and about the punters who come.

14. Judy then says it's time to close and they get up to go. Judy collects her papers, Carol her pole dancing costume and Jackie and Josie give the tables a final wipe down on their way out.

Possible themes to explore

- The ethics of pole dancing
- Men and sex
- The economic circumstances which lead to women working in places like this.
- Shady business dealings
- The economic crisis for small businesses
- Family conflicts
- The Gig economy if Jackie and Josie are on zero hour contracts
- The difficulty for graduates finding appropriate level jobs.

Staging

This was first staged in a bar area so it was easy to arrange the tables to look like a nightclub. Because it was in a bar, we had the option of Josie and Jackie actually serving drinks to the customers / audience.

Props: we got hold of a scaffolding pole and a base for it to slot into. For H&S reasons, none of the women actually swung on the pole. We also needed, glasses, drinks and a sandwich.

3. The Old Biddies

This is a play within a play.

The setting is a B&B where a group of actors on tour are rehearsing a new play.

The play within a play is set in a care home.

All the action takes place in the living room of the B&B.

Cast

Mick & Drew run the B&B with the help of their daughter Jinnie.

Chloe is the Director of the acting company

Kell, Jill and June are three of the actors (also known as the Old Biddies)

Phil is another actor who was once quite well-known but has fallen on hard times

(In the play within a play, these four are residents in the care home.)

Don and Jessie are also part of the acting troupe and are the care staff in the play within a play.

Ashley is the author of the play within a play

Scenes

Scene 1 – breakfast

1.   Don & Jessie enter, looking guilty, see that no one is there and creep back out holding hands

2.   Jinnie enters carrying two plates of food. Calls out "No one's here."

3.   Drew enters: I could swear I heard someone. Put that food back under the grill to keep it warm.

4.   Jinnie leaves, Mick enters. Mick and Drew talk about hard times, how lucky they are to have the actors staying and the need to use the living room as a temporary breakfast room, as the dining room is being painted. Mick leaves with Drew.

5.   Kell and Jill enter – talk about their disturbed night, squeaks in the bedroom next door. Chat about the other actors.

6.   June enters, sits at a separate table. Also complains about the noises emanating from Phil's room.

7.   Chloe enters, bright and cheery. Sits next to June. June complains about Don being given the double en suite room.

8.   Phil comes in next. Goes to sit with Kell & Jill, who say the spare seat is being kept for Jessie. They clearly don't want him to join them.

9.   Drew comes in with Jinnie carrying plates of food. They set them down and leave.

10.   Actors complain to Chloe about how terrible the rooms are and the food is.

11.   Drew comes back in with toast and tea. Chloe airs the complaints. Drew says "What do you expect for the price you paid?"

12.   Drew calls Mick in and asks him to sort out the rooms. They bicker. Mick leaves.

13.   Jinnie enters and starts to clear away the plates. Kell and Jill complain as they haven't finished.

14.   Jessie and Don appear – go to sit at separate tables but there is no room so end up sitting together. Kell and Jill whisper and point at them.

15. Chloe tells people they will be rehearsing after lunch and the author will be coming and he has probably written in another small role. Jinnie who has been eavesdropping drops a plate.

16. Mick walks through, carrying a toilet plunger. Kell calls him over to talk about the lights in her room. He drops water from the end of his toilet brush onto their table. Kell tutts and gets up to leave with Jill.

17. Chloe and Phil have a discussion about the play and the cast. Phil boasts about his previous successes and how he reluctantly joined the company because he values the author's previous works. Chloe has to tolerate his behaviour because she is desperate to have enough actors. They continue talking as they leave.

18. Jessie and Don have a conversation where it becomes clear they are both cheating on their spouses. Jessie is reluctant to continue with this arrangement.

19. Drew enters. Jessie and Don ask for their breakfast. Drew says breakfast is over. Didn't they look at the times. They leave muttering.

20. Jinnie and Drew clear away breakfast things and rearrange room as a living room. Jinnie talks to her mum about wanting to be an actor, how she thinks Phil is great. She is sure she has seen him in something on telly. Drew tries to disabuse her. They leave.

Scene 2: lounge – afternoon

1. Kell, Jill and June are sitting talking about Phil and his habits, including farting and pissing in the wash basin, and how difficult it will be to do a scene where they have to act as if they fancy him. Jinnie is dusting in the background, disgusted and attracted at the same time, as to what they are saying about Phil.

2. Chloe comes in, wonders where the others are. Says this is meant to be a dress rehearsal so why isn't everyone in costume. June says she is.

3. Phil enters, women move around trying to ensure they don't have to sit beside him. Jinnie flutters near Phil. Chloe orders her out.

4. Ashley arrives, saying how important it is that everything goes well, as today is the only rehearsal he can make. Chloe and Ashley have some minor disagreement about the play.

5. Jessie and Don arrive arguing. They stop as they enter the room and try to pretend they are not an item.

6. Mick wanders through carrying some electrical equipment.

7. Chloe says to Jessie and Don they will start with the scene where they are on stage talking about the old biddies. She gets angry with them for not being off script. They bring parts of their offstage argument into how they are delivering their lines much to the author's annoyance. He attacks Chloe for the actors not being ready as it's only two days before the curtain goes up. Chloe turns her anger onto Jessie and Don and tells them to sit in a corner and learn their lines.

8. Chloe says let's try the scene between Phil and the old biddies. At this point, Mick walks through, whistling, much to Chloe's annoyance. Kell and Phil get up – Chloe yells at them for not walking like 90-year old people do. Ashley, yet again, has a go at Chloe for how under rehearsed the play is. The old biddies are reluctant to touch Phil (who lets out a fart at some stage) even though this is what the script calls for. Mick walks back across still whistling. This time everyone yells at him.

9. Chloe calls Jessie and Don back to do the scene where they, as care staff, interact with the old biddies. In this play, someone has pissed their seat and they want to leave it to

the next shift to clean up. Don calls the women 'old codg-
ers'. Ashley jumps up and says the word is 'biddies' and
appeals to Chloe for the actors to keep to script. At this
point Don lets loose a whole lot of derogatory words about
old people. Rest of staff call him to account.

10. Ashley defends his script saying, emotionally, these were
some of the words used to describe his mother when she
was in a care home.

11. Drew comes in and says they need to get out as it's 3.30 and
some of the other residents come in to watch their favourite
afternoon TV programme. Chloe says she booked it with
Mick through to 4.30. Mick walks back in and Drew attacks
him for agreeing to the 4.30 time. There is some negotiation
that results them having the room for two hours in the evening. They all leave. On their way out, Jessie slips Phil a
note.

Scene 3 – evening

1. Drew and Mick come in and talk about how the B&B is on
its last legs and how they are waiting for a phone call from
their estate agent to see if a buyer has come through. They
leave.

2. Jinnie comes in and starts to tidy the room. Chloe comes in
and angrily asks her to leave. She does but stays near the
door.

3. Ashley comes in and asks where everyone is.

4. Jill enters on her mobile phone – 'It's certain then." She
tells Chloe and Ashley that she has just been offered a part
in The Calendar Girls starting next week, so she's off.
Chloe tries, unsuccessfully, to persuade her to stay. Jill
leaves.

5. June comes in with a packed suitcase saying she can't cope
with these conditions – 'they're beneath me.' Argues with

Chloe. While they argue, Phil creeps across the stage and takes Jinnie's hand – they leave.

6. Don and Jessie enter in the middle of another argument.

Jessie: I can't stand it anymore, living a lie, I'm going home to confess all to my husband and I didn't realise you were so ageist.

She leaves and Don follows, still trying to persuade her to stay.

7. Ashley turns on Chloe for hiring such an abysmal group and says he's giving up and going home. He leaves

8. Mick comes in and asks if they've seen Jinnie and why aren't they rehearsing given they made such a fuss about the room. Chloe explains it's all over and leaves.

9. Drew comes in and says the buyer has cancelled – it was going to become a care home but in present circumstances it's no longer viable. Let's go and drown our sorrows. They leave.

10. Kell comes in fully dressed for her part saying 'I'm ready'.

Possible Themes to explore

- Attitudes to ageing
- Use of derogatory language
- Adultery
- Life in B&B's
- Being on the road and what goes on, on tour, stays on tour

Staging

Tables and chairs that can be moved around to create either an adapted dining room or a lounge.

Props:

Breakfast settings – cups, cutlery, saucers, toast, sausages, cereal etc.

A suitcase

A toilet plunger + some electrical equipment

4. The Colander Girls

Cast

Vicar

Vicar's Wife

Caretaker

Reporter

Chris the Photographer

Strippers:

- Cathy – very beautiful
- Jane – an old Windmill girl
- Kim – who believes older bodies are beautiful
- Maddy – Kim's niece
- Dana – photographer's sister
- Jen – initially reluctant

Scenes

1. Vicar and his Wife are on stage discussing the need to raise money to replace the boiler in the church hall. She talks about creating a calendar of their activities but doesn't mention stripping, so her husband believes it will be shots of jam making etc. She tells him a reporter from the local paper is coming to interview her. She leaves to get ready.

2. The Caretaker enters – the Vicar tells him to keep people out of the hall as there will be a women-only meeting taking place. Vicar leaves.

3. Reporter enters – tells the Caretaker that he is meeting the Vicar's wife. Caretaker leaves to get her but as he leaves she enters.

4. The Vicar's Wife and the Reporter discuss the calendar shoot. She wants maximum publicity in order to sell copies. The Reporter is cynical and world-weary and maximizes opportunities to talk about women taking their clothes off.

5. The women arrive:

> Cathy is all up for stripping;
>
> Jen is reluctant;
>
> Kim is up for it on the basis that older women's bodies are beautiful;
>
> Jane being an ex-Windmill girl is also up for it;
>
> Maddy is younger and surprised that older women are up for it.
>
> Dana wants it to happen because it's an opportunity for her unemployed brother to take the photos. She has sold the idea of her brother being the photographer but has simply told the others that she has a relative called Chris who is an experienced photographer.

The women lay out the props (all kitchen equipment including a colander). They try them on, in keeping with their characters. Cathy takes off her bra under her clothes which, during the trying-on of props, slips under the table.

They agree to pose for two months each, though Maddy says she will only do one month.

6. Vicar's Wife arrives – there is a discussion about her role. She is persuaded to do the missing month. They leave to go for a cup of tea except for Dana who says she will wait for the photographer.

7. The doorbell goes and Dana goes and welcomes Chris. They converse and it turns out that he has only done a week's photography course. Dana persuades him it will be OK. Chris talks about life on the dole. He leaves to fetch his equipment, which consists of an old camera as he is too poor to have a smart phone.

8. The women come back in and start to strip. Chris comes back in – the women stop, in protest, as they had assumed he was a woman with a name like Chris. Cathy and Jane are happy to continue, the rest aren't.

9. Vicar comes in – is upset at what he sees – particularly at his Wife taking part. There is a lot of cross talking. As this happens, the Reporter comes back in and persuades Chris to continue filming. The women notice what is occurring and angrily get him to stop. The Reporter slips Chris some money and gets his camera in return, and then leaves.

10. Group turn on Chris and then on Dana, when she tries to defend him. As they are doing this, they are getting dressed and storming out, leaving Dana, Chris, the Vicar and his Wife. Dana mutters her apology and takes Chris off.

11. Finally only the Vicar and his Wife are left – they quarrel, with the Wife arguing she was doing it for a good cause and the Vicar saying her behaviour was unbecoming for a vicar's wife. They leave arguing.

12. Caretaker comes in and starts tidying things up. He notices the bra and picks it up, sniffs it and puts it in his pocket and then leaves.

Possible themes to explore

- Different attitudes towards women's bodies
- What life on the dole is like
- The church in need of money

Staging

Action is centred round a large wallpapering table.

In our performance, the women only partially stripped when trying on the props.

Props: a variety of kitchen utensils – (colander, saucepan, frying pan etc.), a table to put them on, an old-fashioned camera

Relevant Other Publications by Ron Wiener

Acting against ageing: the theatre group helping older people stay creative in The Guardian online newspaper, July 2014

'Notes from a European Workshop: Spontaneity theatre meets sociodrama' in Ron Wiener, Di Adderley & Kate Kirk: *Sociodrama in a Changing World*, www.lulu.com (2011) pp.29-31

'Psychodrama, Theatre and the Community' in *Forum*, IAGP (2006) Vol. 1, pp75-82

'Bradford the Musical – A Producer's View' in *The British Journal of Psychodrama and Sociodrama*, Vol. 20, No.2, pp57-59

'Elders, Drama and the Good Life' in *Quality in Ageing*, Vol. 10, No.4. (2009), pp 49-52

Let's Imagine, www.lulu.com (2012)

Creative Training: Sociodrama and Team Building, JKP (1997)

Co-editor with Di Adderley and Kate Kirk: *Sociodrama in a Changing World*, www.lulu.com (2011)

Co-author with Linda Richmond: 'Acting for a change: Using Psychodrama to Enhance Spontaneity, Connections and Change in the Development of a Senior Improvisation Theatre Group' ASGPP (In Press)